From Inside the Brain of a Dad Looking Out

By Jon Ziegler

Copyright © 2014 Jon Ziegler

Edited by Charla White

Cover design by Jon Ziegler

Cover inset Illustration from

"Magic: Stage illusions and Scientific Diversions"

By Albert A. Hopkins

All rights reserved.

ISBN: 149954538X
ISBN-13: 978-1499545388

DEDICATION

For my wife and daughters who are my inspiration and motivation.

CONTENTS

A Note from the Author	1
1. Here We Go	4
2. I'm So Very Glad to Meet You	7
3. Parental Learning Curve	12
4. Creative Discipline	17
5. Bring On Child Number Two	22
6. Two Steps Forward, Two Steps Back	26
7. Expectations	29
8. Children's Brains Don't Work Right	32
9. Suffering Through the Flu	35
10. How Did We Get Here?	37
11. Hot and Ready	40
12. Murphy's Laws of Parenting	46
13. My Kids Know I'm not Perfect	48
14. Hair by Dad	50
15. It's Mother's Day Already?	55
16. I've Earned the Right	57
17. The Monster Under the Bed	60
18. I Don't Like Your Kids	64
19. Shopping with Children	67
20. A Message from the Natalie Warning System	75
21. The Parents Group	76
22. Things that I Really Hate when They Happen	79
23. I Want More	81
24. Christmas Shopping	83
25. T'was the Night before Christmas	85
26. Absent Mindedness	87
27. Dinner	89
28. What Guys Do Together	93
29. How to Make a Dad Mad	95

30. Parents and Technology	98
31. The Hearing Problems of Daughters	102
32. My Wife has My Back	106
33. Glimpses of Light	110
34. The Worst Best Anniversary Ever	112
35. Rule without Reason	118
36. Has This Ever Happened to You?	120
37. Navigating Parents	122
38. Annoying Trends in Fashion	126
39. Bear Hugs	127
40. Four Non-Morning People	129
41. I'll Take Him	134
42. The Parent Teacher Conference	138
43. Glory Days	143
44. Finances	145
45. The Icy Road Brake Test	148
46. Because I Love Her	155
47. Saturday Night	156
48. A Horrific Tale about Writer's Block	157
49. A Few Helpful Parenting Tips	160
50. Let Me take a Selfie	162
51. Dads, Daughters, and Boyfriends	168
52. Overdose	171
53. When I was Growing Up	176
54. The Power Outage	178
55. Dad Fashion	184
56. A Case of Mistaken Identity	186
57. Will I have Done Well?	190

Stories of Life as Seen Through the Eyes of a Dad.

A NOTE FROM THE AUTHOR

If you have read my first book, *The How-Not-To Guide To Parenting and Marriage,* and have decided to stick around for this, the second book, let me first thank you! It is for you that I decided to write a second collection of silly stories, much like the first book.

What may be slightly different than the first book, is that in addition to all the ridiculous and perhaps slapstick stories that you are familiar with, I also tried to give just a hint more of the honest and introspective thoughts that travel through the mind of a dad, or at least this dad. Again, they are not meant to instruct or provide solutions to the many trials of parenthood and marriage. They are simply thoughts, many without resolution.

This book is meant to amuse my fellow imperfect parents and spouses who may need a humorous break from the stress and anxiety of coexisting with, raising, and surviving life with sons, daughters, husbands and wives.

The stories are designed to play out like little skits, or maybe scenes from a sitcom. Most of them have no deeper hidden meaning or agenda. They are simply offered up as entertainment.

As you read through the stories, you will notice that I sometimes emphasize the worst in our family behavior, mainly because this type of behavior is often what leads to some of the most humorous scenarios that can take place in a household. But in the back of your mind, be aware that my wife and two daughters are the joy of my life. I often fail as a parent and husband, but it is not from a lack of effort to be the best of both. I love my family more than I could ever put into words.

It is because of their love, inspiration, and support that I give you *From Inside the Brain of a Dad, Looking Out*.

From Inside the Brain of a Dad Looking Out

1. HERE WE GO

"I'm pregnant," said the sobbing voice on the other end of the phone.

It took me a minute or so to fully understand the two words that my wife had just told me. "Pregnant" meant baby, someone was going to have a baby. The word "I'm" tacked in front of the word pregnant seemed to indicate that the baby would end up belonging to my wife and I. This was not in the plan for several more years, and judging from my wife's sobbing, I was not the only person to realize this.

"I'm sure it will all work out," came my automated, standard response to whatever situation was currently causing my wife to be upset. But inside my head, a whirlwind of thoughts had been unleashed.

I had always realized that someday, my wife and I were going to have kids. I just didn't realize when I arrived at work that morning that it would be today that our journey to parenthood would begin. We were supposed to be waiting a few years until we got our feet on the ground financially. We were going to have fun and be a care free newlywed couple for a while before we had children. I hadn't even given up on the possibility of becoming a rock star and touring the country with my groupie wife. Having kids "someday" was a lot different than "I'm pregnant."

When you are going to have kids "someday," there is still time to save money and build a house with that perfectly decorated child's room in it. We lived in a small mobile home, and barely had enough money to pay the bills as it was, and on top of that, I had no idea how to raise a child.

Up to this point, my experience with children had been limited to my younger brothers and sister, who I had picked on mercilessly, and a few brief encounters with friends' kids.

There were plenty of times that I would tickle or make a funny face at someone else's baby or child, who would then break into fits of giggling, and cause the child's mother to say something like, "Oh, you will make a wonderful daddy some day!" So I guess I always took it for granted that when the time came, I would simply know what to do. The time was now and I was clueless.

When I really sat and thought about it in the quiet secret places of my mind, I couldn't help but do the math. Kids are a noisy, expensive, disobedient, messy source of stress. Who in their right mind would really want that? I mean, I'm sure there will be times that my 'child to be' will give me moments of joy, laughter and pride. And I truly looked forward to handing them a slice of lemon for the first time to see what kind of funny face they would make when they tasted it. But seriously, was the trade-off worth it? Did anyone truly want to have children? Or was it all just a scam perpetrated by people who had found themselves stuck with kids. Maybe they just figure that if they have to suffer through, they may as well trick other people into making the same mistake.

Making things even worse, it was hard for me to imagine loving my baby. It sounds horrible to say, but without ever having looked at, or held my child in my arms, I just couldn't come up with any genuine affection for it. I didn't even know if it was a boy or a girl yet.

One day as I sat in my living room petting our dog Casey, I couldn't help but think to myself, "I'll never be able to love a baby as much as I love my dog!"

What kind of father loves his dog more than his own child? I shouldn't even be allowed to have kids.

But we were committed now, there was no turning back. So I kept all these thoughts and fears to myself. My wife had plenty of her own fears and concerns to deal with on top of having been turned into a continuous producer of vomit. There was no need to add my insecurities to her misery. I would simply wait until we actually had the child and brought it home before I would tell her that there was no way we could afford diapers, and that we would have to use newspaper instead . . . or make the child live in the bathtub where it could poop and pee at will.

2. I'M SO VERY GLAD TO MEET YOU

It was immediately following a particularly loud clap of thunder that my wife looked at me with horror in her eyes and exclaimed, "My water just broke!"

To confirm her claim, and perhaps due to my not knowing what else to do, I asked how she could be so sure that it was her water that broke, instead of her just peeing in her pants. The look I received indicated that this line of questioning was not appreciated and could possibly result in bodily harm to myself. I decided it might be best to just go with her conclusion that it was indeed her water that broke.

So in the space of a few seconds, all the planning, all the fretting, all the things that still needed to be done were all in the past. This was happening now. I was teetering on the edge between father-to-be and just plain father.

But knowing I had to get my wife to the hospital actually kept me from being as nervous as I thought I would be. In fact, I can honestly say that I hardly thought about the fact that I would soon be a father. Duty and concern for my frightened wife prevented any such ponderings.

The trip to the hospital wasn't nearly as chaotic as it is usually portrayed in the movies or on TV, leaving me feeling like I was overlooking something important. I drove only slightly over the speed limit, and we were calm enough to be able to talk to one another coherently during the ten minute drive.

When we arrived at the Emergency Room, we were whisked away to the baby-having section of the hospital where IV's and beeping monitors were installed on my wife, and we were put in a special baby-having "on deck" room. From the swiftness of how things had gone in the short time we had been there, I fully expected I would be holding my child in time to watch the beginning of the Seinfeld episode on the TV that hung from the wall.

But then for the next hour, things seemed to slow down a bit. Every few minutes, my wife would make sounds of pain as another contraction began. I watched as the graph on the "contraction monitor" slowly rose, mirrored by my wife's noises of distress rising in intensity and then the graph beginning to fall, again in unison with the sounds of my wife's agony.

Her pain was hard for a loving husband to have to endure. It made me feel helpless. I was supposed to be the one to protect her from pain. I would have taken her place if it would have been possible. But at least I was able to reason that her pain would be short lived. The baby should be here momentarily . . . right?

By the third hour, it was growing ever more difficult to listen helplessly while my wife suffered. I would sometimes even lie to her, telling her that the contraction monitor was starting to go back down before it actually did, hoping that if she believed that the contraction was ending, she would feel better.

By the tenth, eleventh and twelfth hours, I was exhausted from the anxiety caused by the waiting and the feelings of being helpless. Contractions were just minutes apart, but in those few short minutes, both my wife and I would fall fast asleep. When the familiar sounds of pain would once again awaken me, I would do my best to comfort her until the contraction had passed and then fall back asleep.

Once we were well into the next day, it was no longer possible to keep track of how many hours we had been there. I estimated we were somewhere in area of sixteen to twenty hours of labor, but I couldn't be sure. We had outlasted two shifts of hospital staff, and latest round of nurses and doctors had just come in to cheerfully introduce themselves. I was frustrated and angry that my wife had been left in agony for so long. I was very close to punching the next doctor or nurse who dared to smile at me.

"If we don't deliver within the next hour, we may consider a C-Section," the current doctor finally said. It was the first thing I had heard in the last twenty hours that seemed to make any sense.

But it was as if the unborn child had actually heard the doctor's ultimatum and decided to get things moving. The doctor who had uttered the words hadn't even finished his exam before things seemed to go up a notch in intensity. Even in my weary, medically ignorant state, I could tell that the time was now.

From out of nowhere, a whole baseball team of gown and mask wearing medical staff entered the room and wheeled us into what I assumed was the delivery room. There was a blur of things happening around me. Medical people were scurrying about, talking in medical language, and my wife was obviously in more pain than the entire previous time spent in the "on deck" room. I stood by my wife's bedside ready to jump in and help anywhere I was needed. But no such requests were coming from the nurses or doctors. Even my wife seemed less than amused with my pathetic attempts to provide her with support. It was undoubtedly clear to me that I was the most useless person in the room. I began to think that the masked baseball team was under the impression that my name was "Excuse me," because that's what they would say every time they needed me to move somewhere in order for them to complete their task. I was simply in the way.

The blur of activity went on for maybe twenty minutes or a half hour. The doctor seemed pleased with whatever was happening down at the "business end" of the delivery, which I guess made me pleased. I certainly wasn't going down there to check. I decided I was much better off staying up at the end that had my wife's face attached, even if that face seemed like it wanted me near her less and less as the pain increased.

Then amongst all the confusion and activity, I heard a sound. A tiny little squeal that didn't even seem human to me. In fact, had I been at home and heard such a noise, I would have already begun to look for some sort of weapon to whop whatever type of rodent was making such a distressed squeal. But then I realized that the squeal was the sound of a baby.

This is where things get a little fuzzy as far as my memory goes. The tiny cry threw everything into a surreal chain of events that I have a hard time recalling with any degree of accuracy. I honestly don't remember if the child was placed into my wife's arms first or mine, but either way, there I was, holding a tiny, slimy baby girl. It was at this very moment that everything changed.

In an instant, all those negative thoughts about not being sure if I could love a baby as much as my dog were gone. The question of money was no longer an issue.

For those few minutes, there was nothing else going on in the world. In fact, I think the world might have actually stopped briefly. All that existed were myself and this tiny little angel. She was perfect. She had a tiny little nose and ears. Her hand was barely big enough to grasp all the way around one of my fingers. And I knew at that moment that no matter how much the cost, no matter how bad raising a child could possibly get, it was all definitely worth it.

I looked down my daughter and quietly said, "I'm so very glad to meet you!"

3. PARENTAL LEARNING CURVE

Now that I had determined that being a father was going to be one of the greatest things that could happen to me on this earth, there was nothing left to do but roll up my sleeves and get busy. There was so much to learn, and so much to teach. And no matter how many books, videos and mother-in-laws you had gotten parenting information from, there was just no way that they could ever cover everything.

You can watch a video on how to change a diaper a thousand times, but until you are there doing it, you really have no idea. No book can prepare you for the assault on your nose once you've cracked open one of these little atomic poop bombs. The smell is actually painful.

A video makes it all look so easy to hold a squirming animal by the feet with one hand, while deftly performing the wipes cleanup and diaper change with the other. But in reality, it's as awkward as trying to write "Metallica Rocks" on your forehead before a concert with a magic marker while looking at the words you are making backwards in a mirror . . . not that I've ever tried to do such a thing. And never, NEVER could I have imagined how many places little girls can hide poop after a really messy one.

Books and videos can't teach you anything about patience either. I mean there will be chapters about it, but until you have been walking, rocking, and singing to a screaming baby for an entire night, you just don't know where your mind will end up going.

Nyquil? No, I'm not sure that's even legal at this age.

Move her crib to the garage? No, that would surely draw criticism from some perfect do-gooder parent somewhere.

Stuff her mouth with a sock to muffle the noise? GOOD LORD, NO! WHAT AM I THINKING! I'm losing my mind! I need sleep!

No matter how much you research, there is only so far a book or video can take you. Some things you will not know about until you have actually done it or dealt with it; feeding, dressing, diaper changing, nap times, formula making, learning how to make that baby burrito with the blanket, all takes experience.

I quickly began prioritizing and categorizing the knowledge that I needed and placed it in order of importance:

1. Things that if done incorrectly or are neglected to be done, will result in the child's death. Such things include feeding, checking on breathing, not driving off with the baby while it's in the car seat that is sitting on the roof of the car after setting it their while you searched for your car keys.

2. Things that if done incorrectly or are neglected to do will result in injury to the child. Such things included letting the infants head bobble around like a punching bag that is being hit due to the child's lack of neck muscles, pushing too hard on the child's "soft spot" because it "feels weird,"

or passing the child around at parties so that friends can take turns touching the child's brain through the soft spot.

3. Things that will not necessarily harm the child, but will earn you the reputation of an irresponsible parent. Such things included putting ball point pen tattoos on the child of skulls, Star Wars characters, and saying's like "Born to Raise Hell," giving the child a slice of lemon to see what funny face she makes when she tastes it for the first time, and putting child into the dryer on a pile of towels in order to freak out the child's grandmother, even though the dryer was unplugged.

Surprisingly enough, another large part of the learning curve for a new parent is learning what things are NOT actually fatal to a baby. As with most new parents, I was constantly afraid of my daughter falling victim to some horrible catastrophe, and in deed, we should be. But after numerous calls to grandparents, doctors, church clergy and poison control centers, I have learned the following list of events and symptoms are not usually causes for panic:

Snot running out of the child's nose.

Child pooping twice in half an hour.

Child giggling and laughing in a manner that convinces her father that she has become possessed.

Child crossing her eyes (as long as they don't stay that way).

Dog licking child's face.

Child licking dog's face.

Child eating a piece of solid food, small bits of crayon, dog food, certain non-poisonous bugs, and even the occasional taste of their own diaper contents (she's quick, and I only have two hands!).

In addition, each child also requires that you not only learn all of the aforementioned, but also demand that you learn all of the unique little idiosyncrasies that every child will develop on their own.

My first daughter had an obsession with pulling peoples hair. This knowledge was particularly useful to anyone with a hairy chest, such as myself, who happened to pick her up without a shirt on. The sudden onslaught of chest hair being ripped out made it actually hard to not drop the child on the floor immediately.

My second daughter had an obsession with the seam at the end of her sock being positioned just right. At first it was infuriating to have to spend the extra minute trying to find the right sock seam position. But I soon learned that the extra time spent initially was a much better deal than her constant complaining and frequently flopping down on the ground to try and fix the seam throughout the rest of the day.

Luckily, learning how to care for a baby or child is not at all like learning something in school. Your desire to learn what is best for your son or daughter is born out of love. It's not like reading through some cumbersome history book full of dates and names that have no real practical application to your own life. This learning is something that you often don't have to force yourself to do. You are learning for a reason. This knowledge concerns the welfare of your child. And unlike school, I never felt compelled to just "wing it" or skip out on my learning responsibilities.

4. CREATIVE DISCIPLINE

One of the greatest debates of the parenting world is the question of what is the proper way to discipline a child. Volumes of books have been written on the subject, millions of lungfuls of air have powered voice boxes in heated debates between parents, counselors, teachers and psychologists.

Does it harm a child to spank them? Does it harm a child not to spank them? Do timeouts really work? The questions go on and on.

With all the debate, I found it hard to settle on what I thought sounded like the most rational theory on effective child discipline. So while my first daughter was quite young, I decided to take the subject in my own direction. I was convinced I could come up with the best possible forms of correction on my own. I was a maverick among parents.

When Hannah was just beginning to learn to walk, I quickly realized that she, like all toddlers, had a tendency to get into things that she shouldn't. My wife's method of teaching her not to do things was to snatch her up, and with a cheerful sounding "no-no, don't touch," carry her off to a timeout in her crib.

Right away, I saw a problem with this method in that Hannah couldn't talk. To her, my wife's correction probably didn't make much more sense than the sound of a car horn honking or a toilet flushing. And besides that, what kind of punishment was a timeout? Who would even think that being sent to your room with nothing to do but take a nap was a bad thing? I wanted to be sent to timeouts! At any rate, I knew I could come up with a much better way.

It occurred to me that I had done a fantastic job at teaching our dog not to poop or pee in the house, so it couldn't be much harder to train a child. I also decided that while my techniques were in the developmental stages, I might be better off not telling my wife until I had perfected them. So I decided not to give any of my ideas a trial run until my wife was not around.

One day, my wife went off shopping with her girlfriends, leaving me home alone with Hannah. This was the chance I had been waiting for. My hypothesis was, the dog responded very well to me cranking up Van Halen at extremely high volumes whenever he pooped on the floor. The scare provided by the painfully loud assault on the dog's ears, combined with a good nose rubbing in the poop, proved quite effective in the house breaking process. So I figured the same method should work on Hannah while teaching her not to touch things she wasn't supposed to . . . well, minus the nose rubbing in poop step. So I popped the Van Halen CD into the stereo and cranked the volume up to maximum level so that I merely had to hit "play." All I had to do now was to wait patiently.

As I sat and watched, Hannah toddled around the living room playing with different toys, and sometimes coming over to me to jabber and laugh at me. She sat down and looked at one of her little books and poked at her obnoxious, electronic music making toy. I was sure that sooner or later she would try to get ahold of something she wasn't supposed too, but I was getting a little impatient.

When she had finished with her music toy, she stood up and headed over to the DVD player. This was it. She was going to play with the buttons on the DVD player, a definite no-no. I grabbed the stereo remote and got ready, my thumb poised over the play button . . . but after a few seconds, she wandered back over to her toys and sat back down. Time was running out. My wife would probably be home before long. And although I was almost certain my new method was fool-proof, I really didn't want to try it in front of her until it had been thoroughly tested.

I decided that to accomplish my trial run, I needed to speed things along a little bit, so I picked up the TV remote, another taboo item, and put it on the floor in front of Hannah. She looked at it, then at me, and went back to her toys.

I went and got the dog's water bowl, one of her all-time favorite no-no's, and set that down as well. Again, she looked at it and went back what she was doing. I was starting to get annoyed that she wouldn't misbehave.

Over the next half hour, I tried multiple forbidden objects, even picking them up and shaking them to entice her to grab one, but to no avail. Frustrated, I sat back on the couch and was about to give up, and then . . . she reached. I couldn't tell exactly which of the objects she was reaching for, but she was reaching. This was it! I grabbed the remote and readied the Van Halen discipline. This could be my only chance. Her hand moved closer to the pile, in the direction of a steak knife, no, the bottle of pills. She was reaching for the bottle of pills!

I raised the remote and plugged one ear with my free hand aannnnnnd . . .

Suddenly the front door burst open, and there stood my wife.

Oh crap.

My wife's mouth opened in shock and she dropped her shopping bags on the floor.

"WHAT IN GOD'S NAME ARE YOU DOING?!"

It suddenly occurred to me how bad the situation must look. I was poised with the stereo remote in hand as I sat watching Hannah reach for a bottle of stool softening pills. On the floor in a ring around her, was the bait pile consisting of remotes, fragile figurines, a couple knives, rat poison, curling iron (which was plugged in and heated up) and an opened bottle of beer. It also occurred to me that I may have gone a little overboard in my enthusiasm.

"I was uhh, I was just trying to teach her . . .

"YOU WERE GOING TO BLAST HER WITH VAN HALEN LIKE YOU DID THE DOG, WEREN'T YOU??!!" she screamed.

"NO, NO . . . well, not as loud . . ."

"AND YOU WERE TRYING TO LURE HER INTO TOUCHING SOMETHING SHE SHOULDN'T WITH ALL THAT STUFF!!!"

"Welllll, she was behaving too well . . ."

"WHAT WERE YOU THINKING?" my wife demanded.

"I just figured that the dog responded so well to the loud music that it might work well on Hannah," I explained feebly.

"So were you going to rub her nose in her own poop too just like the dog?"

"No, that's silly. She's too young to be potty trained yet."

My wife grabbed the stereo remote from my hand and hit me on top of the head with it.

"OWWWW!"

She snatched up Hannah and took her upstairs to get her ready for bed, while I picked up the ring of objects.

When Hannah had been put to bed, I was given an hour lecture on the errors in my thought process, and how could a grown adult treat his own daughter like that, and told me she needed to hire a babysitter for me instead of Hannah.

Although I would have much preferred a timeout to the lecture, I had to admit that she had made some good points. And although I still think it would have worked, I decided that perhaps the Van Halen method wasn't the greatest idea.

Needless to say, creative discipline attempt number one was an epic fail.

5. BRING ON CHILD NUMBER TWO

It seemed like the two years flew by like minutes. I suddenly found myself walking in the very same Emergency Room doors with my wife who was about to have our second child. Only this time, I was a little calmer. I knew right where to go.

Unlike the day to day raising of Hannah who constantly caught me off guard with new situations, I had the child birthing routine down to a science. I know I had actually been through it once before, but that seemed to be all I needed. This was going to be a breeze. Well, not a breeze. I mean there was the issue of my wife being in excruciating pain, but other than that, a breeze.

As usual, or at least the one other time I had arrived at the hospital to have a child, we were whisked away to the baby-having "on deck" room, where multiple IV's, monitors, and wires were attached to my wife. And then once again, things seemed to calm down a bit. I knew from having Hannah that we now had a minimum of fifteen to twenty hours before anything significant would begin to happen, so I turned on the TV and began to search for Star Trek reruns. My wife didn't seem to be very into watching TV; well, I guess she was probably in a lot of pain and all.

After about an hour of watching game shows, because no Star Trek episodes were on, and also holding my wife's hand during any current contractions, I began to get a little claustrophobic.

"I'm going to go explore the hospital for a bit," I casually said to my wife.

Her only response was to cry out in pain as another contraction began.

"Well, I mean after this contraction is over . . . you don't mind do you? I'm sure we've got a lot of time to kill here."

My wife squeezed my hand until I could hear the bones making crunchy sounds, and cursed at me with her eyes. I knew that it must just be the extreme pain.

When the contraction seemed to finally be subsiding, I kissed her on the forehead and headed out the door to the hallway, adding, "Can I bring you a latte?" And then with a chuckle, I closed the door.

I wandered down the hallways of hospital, stopping to chat at some of the nurses' stations and talking to patients sitting in wheelchairs.

"My wife is having our second child," I would offer cheerfully to anyone who would listen, "It's not so bad the second time around . . . well, I mean, other than all that pain she is in."

I continued my meet and greet throughout all the floors and halls of the building, perhaps maybe, losing track of time.

At about the time Richard, from the building maintenance department, had finished giving me a tour of the hospital's boiler room, the door suddenly burst open, and in came an orderly.

"Are you Jon?"

"Why yes," I replied, "my wife and I are having our seco..."

"YOUR WIFE IS HAVING IT RIGHT NOW! WE'VE BEEN TRYING TO PAGE YOU FOR HALF AN HOUR!"

Panic swept over me as I thanked Richard for the tour and then sprinted off down the hallway back to the maternity ward. I suspected I was in trouble.

As I barged into the delivery room, still struggling to get into my sterile gown and shoe covers, I was greeted by several dirty looks from the baby having baseball team. I noticed that they weren't scurrying around like they had while Hannah was being born. In fact, they kind of stood there like there was nothing to do.

And then I heard a tiny little rodent sounding squeal.

My wife sat in bed already holding our very tiny baby girl, Natalie. The look on her face told me that indeed I was in trouble. I had just missed the birth of our second child.

"I'm sooooo sorry," I pleaded.

"Where were you? Why couldn't you hear your name being called on the hallway speakers? Is that hot chocolate on your face?" my wife demanded.

"Well I figured we had lots of time before the baby actually came, so I just went for a stroll around the hospital to meet lots of friendly people, and I had hot chocolate with Wendy in the psychiatric ward, and got to see the boiler room with Richard. I thought this was going to be easy the second time around . . . well, easy except for all the pain you were in."

My wife refused to speak to me for the rest of our time in the hospital. I apologized to her at least twenty-seven times and never entered the hospital room without bringing her a gift of some sort. And I felt disappointed at missing the birth of our second child.

Eventually her anger eased and she once again began talking to me. Although she still, on occasion, refers to our second daughter, Natalie, as the "poor little orphan child." She claims that since she had no husband during Natalie's birth, then Natalie must not have a father.

6. TWO STEPS FORWARD, TWO STEPS BACK

When our second child Natalie was born, Hannah was two years old. I was aware that I didn't know everything as far as being a dad goes, but I figured that my two years' experience with my first daughter would at least count for something. But I soon learned that my two girls were so different even from the beginning that I pretty much had to throw the book out and start from scratch.

Hannah had responded well to the words "NO" being said in a firm authoritative voice. It was sometimes all that was needed to be said. If you said "NO!" loud enough she would puff out her bottom lip and begin crying. Most of the time, situations never went beyond this point.

Natalie was a different story all together. Even after she had learned to talk, the word "NO" didn't seem to register in the child's mind. She would simply look you straight in the eyes, and keep doing whatever it was you had told her "NO.". I even began looking through our book of infant medical conditions to see if one had the symptoms of a child knowing all her words except for the word "NO," but there didn't seem to be any medical conditions with that as a symptom.

She didn't puff her lip out like Hannah when she was upset either. If she didn't like the fact that you had scolded her, she would run up to her room and strip naked. I'm not even sure why, other than to punish us by making us go through the hassle of having to bodily force her clothes back onto her body.

Hannah would draw flowers, people and cars, and learned to read quite rapidly.

Natalie spent her toddler years drawing creepy dogs with three eyes and taking underwear from the clothes basket and putting them around the cat's neck like a collar. Her first words were "bird poop" which she used to communicate everything for at least a week. And she had the equal ability to learn reading, but just didn't have the same interest in it as Hannah did.

Hannah was easy going when it came to what we dressed her in.

Natalie would refuse to wear clothing that she had insisted upon wearing just days prior. Keeping socks on the child was a constant battle due to them "not feeling righ.t"

When it came to potty training, I pretty much just had to lead Hannah into the bathroom and point at the toilet and toilet paper roll. "Sit on this and go, and use that to wipe your butt," was basically all I had to say.

Natalie's potty training involved months of pleading, bribing, and threatening.

There were almost no aspects of child raising that applied to both girls. And it's not like one was any smarter than the other. They are both equally smart, and equally creative.

Once I realized how different they were and that I had to deal with them by taking into account their individual personalities, it became a little easier than trying to force both girls to fit the same mold.

It almost makes me want to have a third child to see what interesting new direction that their personality would take . . . notice I said "almost."

7. EXPECTATIONS

It's funny how we build up expectations about how we think our children should remember experiences and what we feel should be important to them. We are all different and the mind of a child doesn't always work in the way the way that an adult mind does with all our worries and preconceived notions of how things should be.

It can be as simple as the familiar Christmas morning story of watching your three year old unwrap countless bright, flashy, noisy presents that cost hundreds of dollars, only to find out that what they are most delighted with is playing with the boxes that the presents came in.

Or when taking your child to a five star restaurant, only to find out that they are a lot happier eating oyster crackers dipped in ranch dressing than the thirty-five dollar entree that you ordered for them.

A lot of times, it's not only what we think should naturally be a priority in the eyes of our kids, like the expensive presents or expensive food, but what we need them to see as important so that our impact on them as parents is validated. It's hard to watch my daughter play with the vacuum cleaner or boxes instead of all those presents that I spent so much time and money on.

But kids haven't learned yet how they are "supposed" to value things in life. If something is fun to play with, it is simply that, regardless of cost or style or making us feel good about ourselves.

I took my young daughter fishing for the first time. To me, it was a momentous occasion. A father and daughter spending time outside together, the passing on of an activity and skill (debatably) that I have always enjoyed. We spent several hours at one of my secret fishing spots and I was thrilled that she was able to experience catching her first bluegill.

When the outing was over and we returned home to tell mom about the wonderful time I thought I had provided her, I was dismayed to find out that the highlight of her day wasn't the time spent with her father or the joy of catching fish. The thing that she was most impressed with, the one thing that she couldn't wait to tell her mom about was . . . being able to go to the bathroom in the woods.

It's easy to beat ourselves up over our 'failures' to make an impression on our children with the experiences that we think they should treasure. How could I have spent so much effort trying to make a meaningful father-daughter bonding time on our fishing trip, only to lose out to her joy of being able to relieve herself in the wilderness free from the constraints of a bathroom?

But I have learned as they get older, that these perceived failures are not failures at all. They do remember the time we spend with them and it is treasured. When I took her fishing, I expected that she would find the same joy out of the sport that I do, and maybe she did. Fishing was something she had never done before so I assumed that it would be exciting. What I hadn't taken into account, was the fact that being able to pee in the woods was also new to her, and it just so happened that in her world it was more exciting than fishing.

So now, instead of worrying so much about my expectations for what should impress them or whether or not my impact on them is exactly what I think it should be, I celebrate the unique perspective that a child's mind gives us on the world around us. And I have to say, I am learning from them too. They give back a little of my own childhood perspective and wonder. Because after all, peeing in the woods breaks all the rules. Peeing in the woods is freedom. Peeing in the woods is fun.

8. CHILDREN'S BRAINS DON'T WORK RIGHT

When we first had kids, I was under the impression that their brains were empty and all I had to do was fill them with stuff. I figured that filling a child's mind with instructions and information was no different than someone showing me how to operate a new microwave oven. Just push this button, enter cook time, hit start and presto, I now know how to operate a microwave. But I soon found out that with children, it wasn't that easy. I found out that children have something wrong with their brains.

I actually thought that when my daughter was old enough to eat solid food, all I would have to do is stick a fork in her hand and show her how to use it once or twice then we could move on to learning something else. This turned out to be wrong. After a solid hour of showing her how to use a fork, the only thing I had accomplished was getting myself, my daughter and the entire dining room covered in food. I had also suffered a pea to the eyeball and a wad of applesauce being rammed up my nostrils, but my daughter was no better at using utensils than when we started. When my wife walked into the dining room, I expressed my frustration.

"I never knew that children were so dumb! Or maybe it's just our child."

My wife gasped a gasp that I recognized as the "OH NO YOU DIDN'T JUST SAY THAT" gasp.

"Children are not dumb and don't say things like that; especially not about our own daughter!"

I had remembered that my wife frowned upon my calling people idiots, so I thought I would be safe by saying our daughter was dumb, but apparently not.

"Well, think about it. They can't walk, they can't talk, and they crap in their pants. Hannah calls a blanket a MeeMee! It's not a MeeMee, it's a blanket! I mean, I get it that they aren't born knowing all that stuff, but I've been showing Hannah how to use fork for an hour now, and she isn't any better at it than when we began! I don't know what conclusion you would expect me to arrive at other than she is du- . . . stupid."

My wife picked my daughter up out of her high chair and left the room without another word.

I think it was a solid month before Hannah was able to use a fork, and even then not very well.

It seemed like that was how everything went. Learning to walk, talk, and use silverware took weeks . . . months! She didn't even know how to watch TV. It's like she wasn't even aware it was on! Who doesn't know how to watch TV? She would pull the cat's tail and then get bit. I would tell her, "Don't pull the cat's tail or it will bite you!" But the very next day, she would pull the cat's tail again and get bitten again.

But yet, they seem so slow to learn in some areas, and then with other things they learn very rapidly without even being taught. To falsely blame your sister for shampooing the dog with Dijon Mustard and even manufacture the evidence to support your accusation takes a complicated thought process. A complex thought process that they figure out and implement all by themselves. But they can't seem to learn to push down on the shiny silver handle on the back of the toilet to flush it?

It must somehow related to what my wife refers to as "selective hearing" and "selective memory." Only in this case, the kids have "selective learning."

9. SUFFERING THROUGH THE FLU

I woke up this morning with a sore throat and feeling somewhat "achy" all over. I began going through the motions of acting like someone who is distraught over coming down with the flu, but in all honesty my soul was turning cartwheels.

All of you know exactly what I'm talking about. Coming down with the flu is like having a note from your mother that excuses you from any and all responsibilities and duties . . . a note that excuses you from life in general.

Of course, I'm not referring to illnesses that involve frequent bathroom trips or coughing until you pass out. And some colds are just too intense to properly enjoy. But there is that certain range of flu that leaves you just feeling run down and sore, with maybe a slight fever. This is the kind of sick that is second only to a Hawaiian vacation.

You not only don't have to go to work, but you get to lay in bed or lay on the couch all day without feeling guilty . . . an entire day of rest! You aren't even expected to do dishes or fold laundry. And better yet, your spouse will probably bring chicken soup right to your place of rest.

The TV is yours to watch whatever you want. If the kids start to act up or fight, they will be quickly sshhhh'd and removed from the room to allow you to endure your affliction in peace.

And finally, having the flu gives you license to legally indulge in recreational drug use . . . Nyquil.

A few gulps of this nectar of the gods can make any stress or worries disappear into sleepy land, leaving you in a blissful vegetative state. Or, with a slight "accidental" dosage error, the more adventurous flu sufferer can enjoy mild, but amusing hallucinations and loss of motor skills.

So send your "get well" wishes and sympathy, but be assured that my suffering is superficial. If you are really a friend, you will be saying silent prayers that my infirmity lasts an extra day, or maybe even two.

10. HOW DID WE GET HERE?

I remember a time not long ago, when I was the life of the party. I was cool, casual, and I always knew just what to say in every party-type situation. I was fun to be around, and people seemed to genuinely want me to be there. My reason for being on this earth seemed to be party attending.

Now flash forward around seven or so years. I find myself at a party standing red-faced and panting over the sprawled, thrashing body of my four year old daughter. I'm strangling and shaking the child's pink stuffed bunny in my hands violently. The words, "I'LL SET YOUR STUPID MISTER BINKY ON FIRE WITH GAS AND FLUSH HIM DOWN THE TOILET!" have just left my lips only seconds ago at the top of my lungs. Around me are a number of wide-eyed, mouth-hanging-open party goers . . . the same party goers who used to want me at their parties. The room is dead silent other than my panting and my child's maniacal tantrum. Two women, sitting near me lean towards one another and begin whispering. Most likely wondering to each other how I have not had my children taken away from me by now.

So how is it that we got from one reality to the other? What happened in those seven years?

Children. Children are what happened. They have transformed me. They are not growing more mature, it is I who is growing more infantile. I used to be the life of the party. Now I'm the elephant in the room.

Where I used to surf the party crowd, hopping effortlessly from conversation to conversation with ease, I now find myself only getting a few sentences out before feeling the dire need to find out where my daughters are and what or whom they are harming. I used to be calm and collected. Now I'm nervous and sweaty. I scan other people's children whenever they run past for fresh bite marks or missing clumps of hair that resulted from playing with my children. While engaged in conversation, I find it hard to complete a full sentence or two without instinctively stopping to yell, "HAS ANYONE SEEN HANNAH? WHERE'S HANNAH? NATALIE ISN'T WASHING DOLL HAIR IN THE TOILET AGAIN, IS SHE?"

I feel like a zoo keeper who is in charge of a pair of tigers. Only the tigers are not confined to a cage. Instead they are free to roam amongst the zoo visitors, and it is my job to make sure no one gets eaten.

And being at the party, my two tiger daughters are even less apt to actually listen to me than usual. So anything I tell them to do, or not to do, must be said three to five times with an increase in volume each time my demand is repeated.

If it happens to be a party that has the combination of food and nice carpet, I end up nauseous from the stress. I constantly picture myself writing a check to replace the carpet that my daughters have just spilled sloppy Joe and grape Kool-Aid all over. And if anything goes wrong during the party, I assume it was caused by one of my children. I impulsively and furiously begin apologizing.

"I'm sorry about the furnace catching fire, Bill, I'll find out what they did to it."

This is how I find myself standing and panting over my screaming child. The tantrum was caused due to another party-goers child wanting to play with the stuffed bunny that I was now attempting to dismember. My first few attempts to calm her down and assure her that it was ok for someone else to play with Mr. Binky were ignored. In fact, she actually turned up the volume of her fit in response. This is where I once again lost it. And if it was not bad enough that I lost it, I lost it while surrounded by two dozen of my friends during a party, in the middle of the living room, with everyone's undivided attention on my lunatic-like meltdown.

I sometimes wonder if I'll return to normal after the girls are grown and gone. Or will I carry these mental scars for the rest of my life, like a shell-shocked soldier who can't escape the vivid images of war. I fear that even if I am able to return to a normal state of mind after my children are gone, I will have long since eliminated all chances of anyone actually inviting me to their party.

11. HOT AND READY

There was a time while my wife was working a midnight shift at the hospital that I found myself in charge of planning and making all of our dinners. We had always taken turns with the meals, and I actually enjoyed cooking. But when the entire dinner responsibility became my own, I soon became overwhelmed.

At first, it didn't seem like that much of a task. I would simply fry up some hamburgers or make tacos, not a big deal. But as the weeks went by, and I began working longer hours at my job, I soon began to have trouble coming up with meals that everyone liked or finding the time to make them before the girls needed to be in bed. It quickly became a tremendous source of stress.

On one particular day, as I wearily drove home from work trying to figure out what on earth I would make for dinner, I happened to notice the sign in front of a pizza place in town was advertising "Hot and Ready pizzas." Apparently, for $4.99 I could simply wander in, and purchase a medium pepperoni pizza that was already made and just waiting for me to purchase. It seemed a little too good to be true.

A bit skeptical, I pulled into the parking lot and wandered inside. Stepping up to the counter, a pimple faced teenager asked if he could help me.

"Your sign said I could get a medium pepperoni pizza for $4.99," I said with doubt in my voice.

"That's right," was his reply.

"Do I have to buy something else to get the deal?"

"No sir."

Still figuring there must be a catch, I then asked, "How long will it take to make one?"

"No time at all, we have several ready," the teen replied.

"Are these just yesterday's pizzas warmed up?"

"No sir."

"Are they some new miniature version of a medium pizza?"

"No sir."

"Do I have to give you my email address and phone number so you can make the rest of your money by selling them to spammers and phone solicitors who will constantly call and email me?"

"No sir."

I had run out of questions, so I simply said, "I'll take two."

The pimply faced teenager then turned around and grabbed two pizza boxes that were stacked next to another pimply faced teenager who was pulling one pizza after another out of the oven, and placing them in boxes. He then placed the pizzas on the counter and began punching numbers on the cash register.

"That will be $10.59," he said cheerfully.

I stood for a second in disbelief. Surely it couldn't be this simple. But after paying him and grabbing the pizzas, I was forced to admit that it was legitimate.

As I loaded up my pizza deal of the century and drove the rest of the way home, a light was going off in my head. I like pizza. The girls LOVE pizza. I couldn't even fry cheeseburgers for less than ten bucks. And the time and effort it took to walk in and purchase the pre-made pizzas was far less than the effort required to make even the simplest of home cooked meals. Angels began singing in the back of my mind as I realized that this was one of the few times in my life that something was going to turn out even better than I could have possibly hoped.

Arriving at home, I burst in the door and loudly announced, "Pizza!"

Both girls cheered, waking up my wife who was supposed to still be sleeping for another two hours before she had to get up and go to work, which didn't make her happy at all. But it was ok. I was PIZZA DAD! Then, ignoring the complaints of my wife who had been awakened by the pizza cheering, the three of us sat down at the table and joyfully ate pepperoni pizza and sang pizza songs together.

The following day, as I drove wearily home from work, I hadn't even started to consider what I could possibly do for dinner when all of a sudden, there it was again, the sign proclaiming the availability of $4.99 pizzas. For a second I thought, "Well, why not?" But I quickly dismissed such an idea. There had to be something morally wrong with having pizza two days in a row. I had never heard of such a thing. It was simply ridiculous.

But as I drove past the pizza place, I began to contemplate my other dinner options, and nothing came to mind. Certainly nothing that would end up any cheaper, or require less effort. Again, the voice in my head reminded me that I like pizza, the girls LOVE pizza. Whipping the car around, I sped back to the pizza place and ran inside to claim my two medium pepperoni pizzas.

Upon arriving home, I burst in the door and loudly announced, "Pizza!"

The girls squealed with delight! They couldn't believe that they were having pizza two nights in a row. I was the coolest dad ever! Ignoring the complaints of my wife who had once again been awakened by the pizza cheering, the three of us sat down at the table and joyfully ate and sang pizza songs together again.

Three weeks later, as I burst in the door and loudly announced, "Pizza!" I noticed that there was significantly less cheering than the first several times I had arrived home with my pizza bargains. In fact, I'm pretty sure I detected some groaning coming from one of the girls.

It's not like we had eaten nothing but pizza for three straight weeks. I had made sure to actually cook a meal on Wednesdays, and only ordered the incredibly cheap pizzas on the other four days of the week. But still, the girls seemed less than thrilled.

"I don't want pizza, dad," my oldest daughter said in her whiney voice.

"Fine! That just means more for me and Natalie," I said.

"I don't want pizza either, dad. Can I have cheesy macaroni?" Natalie agreed.

Feeling a bit betrayed, I went to the kitchen and put a pan of water on the stove to make macaroni. I opened the box of pizza as I waited for the water to boil.

"Fair weather pizza eaters," I mumbled as I took a huge bite of pepperoni pizza.

As a matter of pride, I was able to finish the slice I had taken from the box. But I had to admit, it was a bit of a chore. As much as I hated to admit it, I was tired of pizza too . . . no, I was sick of pizza.

When the macaroni was done, I took it to the table along with three plates. I dished some up for both girls, and then for myself.

"Dad?"

"Yes, Natalie," I answered.

"This is the best cheesy macaroni I've ever had."

After finishing the bite that was in my mouth, I smiled and said, "I think you are right, Baby Girl."

I'm not so sure it was the macaroni that was so good as much as it was the fact that it simply wasn't pepperoni pizza. It was decided that night at dinner that we would take a break from pizza. A decision that had both girls cheering as enthusiastically as they had the first night I had showed up as Pizza Dad. I must admit that although I don't think it would be possible for me to eat another piece of pepperoni pizza, I was saddened by the loss of my cheap and easy meal.

It's now been two months since the last time I had brought pizza home for dinner, and neither girl has asked for it yet. I was back to the routine of trying in vain to come up with meals that everyone liked. Then, one day as I was driving home from my long tiring day of work, a sign caught my eye that read, "Tacos $6.99 a dozen."

12. MURPHY LAWS OF PARENTING

Your turn to change the diaper will always be the poopy one.

No, she will never wear the 400 dollar prom dress again.

Every child will at least once in their life, date someone who is just like yourself at that age . . . and you will hate them.

Yes, it needs batteries, and no, no matter how many times you look, they still weren't included.

No matter what you do, or how you do it, there will still always be someone who thinks that you are a horrible parent.

It needs stitches.

No child under the age of 10 will make it to the toilet to throw up and if given the choice, they will always puke on the carpet instead of the linoleum.

No matter how many times you put the car seat in, you still won't know how to do it the next time.

You will not hear about the science project they were assigned until the day before it is due.

Approximately 32% of the clothing you buy for your children will be worn for the first and last time in the department store changing room. They will spend the rest of their existence in the "I don't like to wear that" pile in the bottom of the child's closet.

They will need braces and your insurance won't cover them.

They will need glasses and your insurance won't cover them.

Your child will be the one picking their nose or wetting their pants in the middle of the church Christmas program.

During the time your kids are growing up, you will repeatedly threaten to send them to Siberia, sell them to the gypsies, let them starve to death, or hope they freeze to death for not wearing a coat. But after they are grown and gone, you will spend the rest of your life missing them.

13. MY KIDS KNOW I'M NOT PERFECT

If you have made it this far into the book without stopping and demanding your money back from wherever you purchased it, then it is not a surprise to you when I say that I am not a perfect dad. In fact, I'm far from it. And believe it or not, my daughters are also aware that I am not perfect.

There is no such thing as a perfect parent. And there are no children who aren't aware of their parents' shortcomings. They see that we can be a little too quick to anger. They see when our own selfish interests push things that are important to them to the bottom of our priority list. They feel it when we are annoyed by them just being kids.

There are so many things I could improve on as a dad, and there are so many dads out there who are doing a better job than me. But the one thing I have always taken great care to maintain is recognizing and admitting when I was out of line and then trying to improve on it. I suppose that would make me weak in the eyes of parents who are under the false impression that they have it all figured out.

If I lose my temper and act disproportionate to whatever they had done to cause my anger, or if I minimize something that is very important to them, I will go back and apologize. I'm not afraid to tell my girls, "I'm sorry, I shouldn't have done that."

If I try to act as if I can do no wrong when it comes to being a dad, my daughters will know that I am a sham and then I lose credibility. To own up to the faults that they already know I have, shows them honesty. Beyond that, I want them to learn that taking inventory of our actions and opinions is an important step in self-improvement. After all, you can't fix what you won't admit is broken.

14. HAIR BY DAD

I had never really given my daughter's hair very much thought. My wife had just always taken care of that department. It never really occurred to me that this was a part of taking care of little girls . . . that is, until my wife decided she was going to spend a week with her mother, who had fallen ill, in Ohio.

During her preparation for the trip, my wife repeatedly asked if I thought I could handle the care of our four and six year old girls while she was gone. The suggestion that I might not be capable was beginning to grate on my nerves. Did she think I was a complete idiot?

"I'll be fine!" I demanded. It's not like I was some dad who was never around to share in the responsibilities of raising and caring for our children.

After several reassurances that I was more than fit for the job, she finally finished her packing and on Saturday afternoon, departed for Ohio.

The remainder of the weekend went fairly smoothly in light of my wife's absence. There was only one incident involving the dog, hairspray, a curling iron, and a few moments of strife over my dinner offerings (which I quickly solved by appeasing the two picky eaters with substituting the meatloaf that my wife had suggested with a dinner of Fruity Pebbles and popcorn). I began to think that parenting solo was even easier than I had thought it was going to be . . . until Monday morning.

On Monday morning I awoke early and began preparing a breakfast of Fruity Pebbles and leftover popcorn. As I was setting out the spoons and bowls on the dining room table, my oldest daughter appeared in the doorway of the dining room looking very much like a girl who had just stumbled out of bed.

When I had insisted that I was more than capable of taking care of my girls while my wife was gone, I was fully aware that part of my duties would be getting the six year old, Hannah, ready for kindergarten. But it wasn't until the very moment that she appeared for breakfast, that I actually realized that this involved doing something with her hair. Once I realized that I had to do something with her hair, I then realized I had absolutely no idea how to do my daughter's hair. It was, perhaps, the only child care duty that I had never actually taken part in.

Quickly, I grabbed the rather lengthy child-care manifesto that had been authored and stuck with a magnet to the refrigerator by my wife. It contained detailed instructions on meal plans, day by day outfits for both girls, and a list of fifty-seven "do's and don'ts," but no instructions on hair. For a few seconds, I felt the horrible grip of panic begin to sweep over my frantic mind.

"I can do this!" I said aloud as if it was necessary to convince myself. After all, if I could figure out how to resuscitate a gravely ill lawn mower or fix the dishwasher with parts from an obsolete pool pump, I could surely figure out how to do a six year olds hair. So after breakfast, I marched my little ragamuffin into the bathroom, and sat her up on the vanity.

Her hair, other than being clean from a shower the night before, looked much like a hurricane survivor's hair. It had a sort of wild frizz on the top and back, and the left side was sticking straight out from her head. The right side was matted flat from being slept on and refused to "re-inflate" with my attempts at fluffing it.

"How does mom do your hair?" I asked, hoping to at least gain some direction.

"With these," my daughter answered, holding up a handful of hair restraint objects.

"AHA!" I exclaimed, grabbing the bands, clips and barrettes from her little hand.

I decided that the easiest and most effective method of attacking her hair would be a simple pony tail. So I grabbed the largest handful of crazy hair I could manage, I wrangled it into one of the elastic holders that I had gotten from my daughter.

"OOWWWW, DAD!" yelled the little person, turning to face me.

Her eyes had been drawn open as wide as two eyes could possibly be opened from the tightness of the pony tail holder, which gave her a surreal, ghoulish appearance.

"Oh, sorry Baby Girl," I said loosening the holder a bit, which allowed several of the wild clumps of hair to escape.

Once I was satisfied that the pony tail was fairly centered on the back of her head, I set my sights on dealing with the hairs that had found freedom when I loosened up holder. To accomplish this, I utilized everything I had in my hair arsenal.

For most of the areas that seemed determined not to be tamed, I was able to handle using a few bobby pins and a can of hairspray. I developed a method of spray and smooth first, and then add a bobby pin if I felt the particular group of hairs might rebel later on in the day. The final two extra stubborn "trouble areas" I resorted to a few pieces of transparent Scotch tape, which were quite effective, and only noticeable with close inspection.

"Done," I proclaimed triumphantly, and held up a mirror for the child to inspect my work.

Hannah looked at her hairstyle for long minute, turning her head from side to side.

"There," she said, pointing to one particularly stubborn spot of wild hair that refused to lay down peacefully.

Searching through one of the drawers in the vanity, I found a pair of scissors and snipped the offending hairs off tight to her head. With a few more seconds of looking in the mirror, she seemed satisfied and hopped down from the sink top.

I was quite proud of my accomplishment, especially in light of never having dealt with one of my daughters' hair before. It didn't even look that bad from a distance. I figured as long as she didn't walk under an extremely strong electric magnet causing the couple dozen bobby pins to be removed, I might have just pulled it off. Better yet, my wife was not here to point out any of the minor imperfections. I couldn't help but feel a sense of victorious jubilation as I loaded Hannah and her sister into the car and headed off to school.

Upon arriving at school, the three of us walked to Hannah's classroom where we were met at the door by her teacher, Mrs. Stanford.

"Well good morni . . . Oh my!" her teacher said, causing me to doubt my hair styling a bit. "Is mom out of town by any chance?"

"As a matter of fact she is," I answered as I realized that the bright lights of the classroom made the many layers of hairspray and pieces of tape considerably more noticeable. "But I figure she doesn't really need to be concerned with all the details of how things went without her," I added with a hopeful wink.

"Oh, I've been around. You are not the first dad to deal with a daughter's hair in mom's absence," she said reassuringly, and then said in a cautious voice, "you do know that . . . uhhh . . ."

"Know what?" I asked impatiently.

"You do know that it's picture day, right?"

15. IT'S MOTHERS DAY, ALREADY?

It's Mother's Day? How can it be Mother's Day? Wasn't it Mother's day a few months ago? Or maybe that was Valentine's Day or Christmas or something.

Nevertheless, it's I-do-love-and-appreciate-you-but-as-usual-I-forgot-to-buy-you-something-that-proves-it day.

The girls and I are on full scramble alert. They know the routine well, as it comes several times a year on Valentine's Day, Mother's Day, my wife's birthday, and occasionally even on Christmas.

Natalie will rummage through the refrigerator and cupboards to find whatever she can to make up one of her notorious breakfasts in bed for the wife/mom. She had become a master at pulling together a four-star feast from whatever grocery and leftover remnants that happen to be in the refrigerator and cupboards. Past breakfasts in bed have included a bowl of chocolate chips, Flamin' Hot Doritos, leftover pizza and even old Halloween candy.

With the excuse of needing to run to the store for toilet paper, Hannah and I take the opportunity to make a flying trip to Meijer during said breakfast, to grab some flowers, a card and maybe a necklace that has a butterfly or some hearts on it. And then return home to wrap the presents with newspaper or place into a re-gifted gift bag that is adorned with a Hello Kitty design.

My wife is awesome. Each time the morning panic of a forgotten holiday ravages our house and the banging of cupboards signals that she is about to enjoy one of the most horrible breakfasts in bed's she has ever had, she gracefully pretends to not know what is happening. She will cheerfully eat her Mother's Day breakfast and act overwhelmed with joy over our gifts every time . . . and that is why I love her.

16. I'VE EARNED THE RIGHT!

My daughter, Natalie, came bounding down the stairs, just as I was opening my mouth to shovel in another heaping spoonful ice cream. She was supposed to be in bed.

"Hey, how come you get ice cream and we didn't?" she screamed.

"Because!" I answered, not knowing what else to say.

"Because why?" she persisted.

Franticly, I searched for an answer to the question that would end the conversation without further explanation, but I was having a little trouble coming up with one.

Finally, not knowing what else to say, I yelled, "Because I've earned the right to! Now go to bed!"

Much to my surprise, she turned around and ran back up to bed.

Proud of myself for coming up with a reason that had diffused the situation without another word being spoken, I went back to eating my ice cream, which tasted even better now than it did before my daughter had caught me.

A few minutes later, my daughter appeared again on the stairs with her older sister, Hannah, standing beside her.

"We want to know why YOU get ice cream and we don't!" said the eldest daughter.

I realized that my victory celebration was a bit premature. My answer hadn't satisfied my daughter like I thought. She wasn't running back upstairs to go to bed, she was going to get her lawyer.

I could have ended the whole episode by giving them each a small bowl of ice cream and then sending them back up to bed. But then again, it was the principle of it. I HAD earned the right to sit and eat a bowl of MY ice cream in MY house without having to explain it to a five year old and her seven year old lawyer . . .so I went off.

"Because I work hard all day so that I can pay for this ice cream as well as all your clothes and food and toys! I'm a fully grown adult AND your father. I've earned the right to eat a bowl of ice cream after you two go to bed, just like my dad did when I was a kid! I've earned the right to walk outside in my socks and still yell at you for walking outside in your socks! I've earned the right to not eat Lima beans! I've earned the right to put my elbows on the table, and say things that you aren't allowed to say! And I've earned the right to not be questioned by you two little people about my eating a bowl of ice cream!!!"

When I was finished with my rant and panting from the exertion it had required, my daughters stood looking at me with their eyes wide and mouths open. Without a word, they both turned and ran back upstairs.

"HA!" I exclaimed triumphantly and continued eating my ice cream.

But by the time my spoon was clanging against the bottom of the empty bowl, the "big old softy" side of my role as dad was starting to tug at my conscience. I felt bad about yelling at my girls and realized that there wasn't a child alive who wouldn't complain about someone eating ice cream in front of them.

Disappointed in my own perceived weakness, I scooped out two small bowls of ice cream and took them upstairs to the room my daughters shared. Both girls cheered with delight as I handed them each a bowl and told them, "lights out as soon as you are finished."

As I came back down the stairs and took my seat back on the couch, my wife, who had been witness to the whole episode, turned towards me and smugly said, "You might have the right, but you don't have the heart."

17. THE MONSTER UNDER THE BED

One night, when I walked into five year old Natalie's room to tell her goodnight, I noticed that the child was crouching on the edge of her bed, looking down to the floor as if she were waiting for something to come out from under her.

"What on earth are you doing, baby girl?"

"There's a robber under my bed," she stated matter of factly.

With a chuckle, I assured her, "There is no robber under your bed. I don't think anyone could even fit under . . ."

But before I could finish my sentence, I heard it. From under the bed, there came a faint rustling sound and then a "clunk." I felt my eyes get big as I shot a look at Natalie, who returned it with an expression that clearly said, "I told you."

In what must have been a brief moment of panic, I lost track of just how it came to be that I ended up crouched on the edge of the bed next to Natalie, looking down at the ground as if we were waiting for something to come out from under us.

After a few tense minutes and a few more noises from under the bed, my older daughter Hannah wandered into the room and looked at the two of us inquisitively.

"What are you guys doing?" she asked.

"There's a robber under the bed," my youngest answered.

Hannah looked at me for some clarification.

"Umm, I don't think it's a robber . . ." I started to explain cautiously.

"There's a monster under the bed," Natalie then added.

Again Hannah looked at me.

With a shrug of unsureness, I tried to prevent the situation from elevating to sheer terror, "Well, I'm not going to say that I think there's a monster under the bed, but . . ."

The clunking noise once again came from underneath the bed. In a flash, Hannah took her crouching place next to me and Natalie on the edge of the bed, all three of us looking at the floor as if we were waiting for something to come out from under us.

Hannah turned to me and with a fearful voice said, "It's a monster isn't it?"

For a second I tried to formulate a less scary explanation for the noises that were emanating from under the bed, but I had nothing. The clunk was far too heavy to be a mouse.

"Yes, it might be a monster," I was finally forced to admit to my daughter.

One of the unfortunate aspects of being a father in a situation such as this is that both of my daughters sat wide-eyed and silently staring at me, waiting for me to figure out how to save the three of us. My brain scrambled, trying desperately to come up with a solution, while simultaneously doing my best to suppress the rising sense of horror that I was beginning to succumb.

I realized that my cell phone was in my pocket, so I pulled it out and speed dialed my wife, who was downstairs watching American Idol . . . completely unaware that her husband and two daughters were trapped upstairs facing certain death.

"Hello?" she answered in a somewhat bewildered tone, "aren't you upstairs?"

"Yes, I am. I need you to go to the basement and get one of the softball bats and bring it up here . . . or a butcher knife, either one, and don't ask!"

"What are you talking about?" she said sounding curiously annoyed.

"Please just do it," I plead without trying to sound frantic.

I could hear her moving around downstairs and grumbling about having to get off of the couch. I heard the kitchen drawer open and close, followed by the sound of my wife coming up the steps.

"What is going on up here?" she demanded as she entered the room.

"There's a monster under the bed." Natalie explained quite calmly.

My wife looked at Hannah, who nodded in agreement, and then at me.

"Welll, I'm not going to go so far as to say that it's a monster under there, but there is something."

Right on cue, the rustling and clunk sound started up again. My wife's gaze focused on the underside of the bed.

Without a word, she walked over to the edge of the bed and squatted down to look underneath our perch. She then let out a disgusted snort and reached under the bed. The three of us on the bed gasped and hid our eyes. A mild scuffle could be heard, and then she pulled her arm back out and held up CeeCee, our large Persian cat.

With a sigh of relief, the three of us were able to get off the edge of the bed. In addition to relief, I also felt a bit of embarrassment over having been saved from a "monster" by my wife.

"So you thought there was something under the bed, and called ME to come up and deal with it?" my wife demanded. "Were you thinking that it would be better for me to get attacked by the monster instead of YOU?"

"That's why I told you to bring up a weapon," I answered pathetically. "I figured if you had a bat or a knife, you might fare better than the three of us who were unarmed!"

Ever since the whole monster under the bed incident, my wife seems to delight in telling the story, shedding a most unflattering light on my role in the situation. I have since vowed that no matter what type of horrible beast is haunting our house, I would much rather be eaten alive, than to give her any more ammunition for degrading stories such as this one she enjoys telling.

18. I DON'T LIKE YOUR KIDS

I've finally realized that when you really get down to it, I don't like other people's kids. I pretend to because that's what we are expected to do. But in all reality, I find other people's kids more annoying, less intelligent and much uglier that my own. My kids are adorable and are "really advanced for their age." When they do things wrong, it is because they just don't understand all the consequences of their actions yet. But I just don't see it in other people's kids. And to be fair, I often suspect that other people just don't see it in mine.

We all fake it quite well. We get together as friends and boast about our children's latest accomplishments and then politely listen to our peers boast about theirs, but if there was a loud speaker on top of our heads that broadcasted our thoughts, we probably wouldn't all be friends any more. The typical parent to parent conversation would probably sound something more like this:

Other parent: "Mackenzie can say her ABC's and count to one hundred!"

Me: "Oh wow, she must be advanced for her age."

Loudspeaker: "Mackenzie can say her ABC's? You mean the same Mackenzie that was over there ten minutes ago eating dog food out of the dog bowl without a stitch of clothing on? Oh yeah, she's a real genius."

Or

Other Parent: "Cody is a natural at football. I think we might have an NFL quarterback here!"

Me: "Yes, he does seem to have a lot of energy."

Loudspeaker: "Little Cody is a delinquent, and has already been expelled three times in his short school career. The only thing he might actually succeed at is having a good sales record at the meth lab he will operate out of your basement when he's thirty-seven."

And although we never say it, things that are common to all kids seem to be no big deal when it comes to our own children, but are unbearable when other people's kids are concerned. Other kid's poopy diapers smell much worse. The snot running down their nose is much grosser. Their voices are whinier and their intentions are much more sinister.

If there is a dispute between our children that boils down to the conflicting testimony of one child against the other, my child is obviously telling the truth and your child is obviously lying. After all, I know my kids and they would never lie to me.

If my kid hits your kid, it's because he doesn't understand that he's hurting your kid, besides your kid probably provoked him. He's really kind and gentle. There is just no way that my darling child would ever purposely harm another human being.

But if your kid hits my kid, he's a monster who needs medication and counseling, and is obviously the victim of horrible parenting skills.

I guess maybe a lot of this type of thinking might be a symptom of our own insecurities as parents and maybe we are just used to the smell of our own kid's poop and not the smell of other kids. It's not like I hate other kids. I try hard to see my friends' children in the same light as my own. But the fact remains, that they just aren't my kids.

So please don't be offended when I say I don't like your kids, it's truly nothing personal. And be assured that I understand if you don't have all that much affection for my own children, even if you are polite enough to not say so.

19. SHOPPING WITH CHILDREN

Even before our children were born, my wife and I had decided that she wouldn't work until both girls were at least in school. We felt that those first five or six years were very important in a child's development, and didn't want those years to be spent in a daycare.

During those first few years, I often worked long hours to make up for the loss of one income, and as a result, I wasn't always aware all of the day-to-day details of raising two active young girls.

My chance to experience many of these daily triumphs and tribulations came one fall when my wife ended up coming down with a particularly bad virus that left her incapacitated for nearly a week. During her recovery, I decided to take a few days off from work to fill in as the child minder.

In the middle of that week it became necessary to do some grocery shopping, so without a second thought I made up a list and informed my wife that the girls and I would be going shopping.

"You're taking the girls?" my wife asked in a concerned tone.

"Yeah, that way you can relax without having to worry about them."

"Are you sure you know what you are signing up for?" she said, with an even more worried tone.

I began to get a little annoyed at her lack of confidence in my child management skills. I realized that taking a three and five year old pair of girls to the grocery store would require vigilance, but come on, how hard could it be?

"You just relax, I've got this," I said as the girls and I walked out the door.

The short drive to the grocery store was uneventful and further confirmed in my mind that this shopping trip was a cinch.

Upon arrival, I grabbed a shopping cart and put three year old Natalie in the little flip down seat, and let Hannah take a spot riding on the front of the cart. I dug out my shopping list to have in hand as we headed down the first aisle.

Half way down the first aisle, I turned to place an item in the cart, only to find Natalie was holding a bag of navy beans that I hadn't placed in the cart.

"Where did you get that, baby girl?" I chuckled as I took the bag from her.

Natalie answered with a blood curling scream that actually made me jump a little.

"DAD! She WANTS the beans!" Hannah advocated from the front of the cart.

"Well, we are not buying beans today," I said in my firm dad voice and put the beans back on the shelf.

As I made the turn from the first aisle to the second, I mentally noted that I should keep the cart centered between the two rows of shelves to prevent my little grocery thief from being able to grab items off of them.

When I got down to the pasta section, I noticed that the brand of lasagna noodles that my wife normally purchased seemed to cost significantly more than a few of the other brands. But it was hard to know exactly how much because the packages contained different amounts of noodles. So I got out my phone and used the calculator on it to try and figure out what the cost per pound would be of each brand of noodle. After a bit of difficulty remembering just how to set up such a calculation, I finally determined the costs of each.

"HAH!" I exclaimed triumphantly, "This brand is seventeen cents cheaper per pound."

I grabbed the new bargain brand of lasagna noodles from the shelf and turned back towards the shopping cart. Hannah was now sitting inside the cart digging into a freshly opened box of cereal that I had gotten from the first isle in what I assumed was an attempt to get to the prize. Cereal was spilling out of the box and onto the floor through the holes in the bottom of the cart.

"HANNAH! What on earth are . . . WHERE'S NATALIE?" I said in a panic as I realized that my youngest daughter was no longer a passenger on the shopping cart.

"She went to get lunch," Hannah replied as if it was not a big deal.

"Does mom let her go get lunch when she takes you guys shopping?"

Hannah looked up from her cereal box digging for a moment and replied, "No, mom doesn't let us out of the cart."

"Oh crap!" I thought aloud sprinting down the aisle.

When I reached the end, I was able to determine that my daughter had gone to the left by the trail of navy beans left like breadcrumbs. Up ahead I could see her standing in front of a lady handing out samples of some sort of food she was promoting. The lady had given Natalie what looked like a chicken nugget and Natalie was busy dowsing the nugget with ranch dressing from a bottle that I had no idea how she came to possess.

"NATALIE! I didn't know where you were!" I said scooping her up, nugget, ranch dressing and all. Natalie screamed once again and stiffened her body in protest of my picking her up.

"She seems quite hungry," the teen-aged sample girl said with a smile, "she's eaten five of my samples."

But I didn't have time for niceties, I had to get myself and Natalie back to the cart before Hannah disappeared as well. So once again, I began to run back towards the aisle where I had left the cart and my treasure hunting daughter. But my progress was hampered by a child who was not happy about being torn away from her free lunch. I had never realized until that moment, how difficult carrying an unwilling child was compared to carrying one who was a willing participant. It was very awkward, much like running with a large, screaming piece of plywood in my arms.

When I reached Hannah and my cart, I stuffed the still screaming Natalie back in her seat and pushed on at a faster pace ignoring the fact that Hannah was still sitting inside the cart. I hoped that picking up the pace was the key to a successful shopping trip with the children by not giving them as much time to get into mischief. However, this didn't end up helping much at all.

By the time I had finished the second aisle and had gotten only half way down the third, Natalie had escaped another two times from her seat in the cart, helping herself to a box of animal crackers and knocking a jar of pickles off a shelf causing it to shatter across the floor. Hannah had successfully found the prize in the cereal box, which was a whistle and blew it loudly from her place inside the cart.

And all I had to show for all the chaos was a half-eaten, half spilled box of cereal, a loaf of bread and a bottle of liquid cold and flu medicine. I was beginning to feel light headed from the anxiety . . . but I had to press on. I could do this.

I grabbed Natalie once again and plowed my way down the rest of the third aisle and into the fourth, picking up a store employee with a mop, bucket, and broom who had been assigned to follow us around by the manager.

Progress was slow and with each stopping of the cart brought a new disaster. I chased girls, put smuggled items back on the shelves and apologized to other customers who had become victims of items thrown or splashed on them. As I turned and looked back down aisle four, it looked like a road map of where my cart had traveled. The path had been clearly marked by a peanut butter wheel track and each stop punctuated by a spill.

I was quickly losing my grip on sanity as we made our way down aisle five. To keep Hannah occupied, I had given into her demand to push the cart. I had restrained Natalie in her seat with the seat belt that I had discovered. The employee with the broom and mop had been joined by a manager who followed along keeping a running tab of items broken. Natalie was like a demon possessed wild cat, screaming and clawing at people who passed by us.

As I walked back to return a customer's purse that had been swiped from a cart we had parked next to in the canned vegetable section, I was startled to hear the scream of someone other than my two daughters . . . the scream of a lady.

Hannah had pushed the cart full force into the heels of an elderly lady, who now sat on the floor crying. The manager was dividing his time between seeing if she was ok and lecturing me on controlling my children. The employee with the broom was sweeping furiously, trying in vain to keep up with the handfuls of sugar that Natalie was throwing on the floor . . . that's when things get fuzzy.

I can remember a period of time with people yelling at me, children screaming and food being thrown, but it was all a blur. My mind had checked out.

After an undetermined amount of time in this confusing dream like state, the spinning of the room began to slow a bit as I gathered my wits about me. I found myself standing inside the shopping cart with the bottle of cold and flu medicine in my hand. The bottle was open, and apparently I had chugged half of its contents while singing "Amazing Grace" in a high falsetto voice. Around me stood the store manager, the still furiously sweeping employee, and the elderly lady who was still crying. Natalie was a short distance away sharing a box of cookies with another customer. Hannah was standing on the front of the cart holding a half-eaten carrot between her fingers like a cigar and moving her eyebrows up and down Groucho Marx style.

"You're funny Dad," Hannah giggled.

After quickly writing a check to cover all food items that had been spilled, damaged, and eaten, I grabbed both girls by the hand and exited the store, leaving the cart sitting in the exact same spot where I had just used it as my stage.

Arriving at home, I unloaded the girls from their car seats, and with the Chinese take-out I had picked up, went into the house.

"Where's the groceries?" my wife asked, "Was there a problem?"

"Nope! Theeee . . . ahhh grocery store was closed, "I managed to fabricate.

"Why didn't you just go across town to Leonard's Grocery Store?"

"Uh, well that was closed too. I think it was some sort of grocery store holiday."

To stop the obnoxious line of questioning, I brought my wife a heaping plate of sweet and sour chicken, and then sat down with my own plate, still reeling from the effects of the cold and flu medicine.

After a few minutes of silent eating, my wife said, "By the way, the manager of the grocery store that was closed called."

I stopped my eating with the fork of food hovering just outside my opened mouth.

"Oh?" I said sheepishly.

"It seems he failed to charge you for the live lobsters that were apparently killed by somebody dumping some sort of blue liquid into the tank."

I was busted. "Well . . . that explains where the fabric softener went."

20. A MESSAGE FROM THE NATALIE WARNING SYSTEM

Attention all animals residing in my house!!! This is a message from the Natalie warning system:

Natalie (the young girl that also lives here and who treats you all like her children) has recently determined that all of you smell and have greasy fur. Those of you that have been with us for a while knows that this means that at some point in the next 24 hours, your flea-bitten carcasses will be snatched up, and hauled into the bathtub, regardless of any snarling, hissing, teeth gnashing, and claw baring. You will be thoroughly scrubbed, have your fur styled and fumigated with smelly-goody stuff.

It is useless to resist.

Do not look to me for help. I will be going to the neighbor's house when the melee begins, and will not be returning until the baths are over and the hair and blood stain cleanup phase has begun.

You have been warned.

21. THE PARENTS' GROUP

I went with my wife to a parenting group in hopes of figuring out how to fix our children. When we arrived at the place where the group meetings were to be held, we went in and sat down. I had a pen and notebook so that I wouldn't miss any good ideas on children fixing.

As the parenting group began, it didn't take long for me to realize that the main objective of the group was to fix the parents. I figured that I didn't need any fixing. Obviously we had come to the wrong group, or simply hadn't understood the purpose of the parenting group, so I got up to leave.

"Is something wrong?" asked the disturbingly cheerful group leader.

"Oh, no, I just thought this was a group about how to fix our kids, but it seems to be as much or more about fixing us as parents. My wife and I don't need all that much fixing," I replied.

With a patronizing smile, the increasingly obnoxious group leader then said, "Well, Mr. Ziegler, we find that most behavioral problems that aren't physiological or psychological originate, or at least can be corrected by educating the parents on better parenting concepts."

With a teen-like roll of my eyes, I continued towards the door, at which point, my wife caught up to me, and standing in my path, said that I needed to sit back down.

We began to argue loudly and with flailing arm gestures, and me plugging my ears at times while yelling, "I CAN'T HEAR YOU, I CAN'T HEAR YOU!" (This probably confirmed to the other members of the group that we both needed fixing.)

My wife, seizing the opportunity, shouted, "How can you say that you don't need fixing when you are acting just like they do?"

"Well I'm not the one who is constantly nagging them about stupid things like burping and farting at the dinner table! It's no wonder that they are messed up!" I shot back.

"NO! You are the one who is encouraging the burping and farting at the dinner table even though you know it makes me angry!!"

I yelled, "I'LL FIX THE WHOLE PROBLEM BY GLUING THEIR HAIR TO THE REFRIGERATOR DOOR!!!"

A collective gasp could be heard throughout the members of the group. I realized that my statement probably wasn't the best choice of words when trying to convince a parent's group that I didn't need any fixing. In fact, I wasn't even sure where I had come up with that idea.

After several very loud minutes, and the group leader doing his best to mediate with a pleasant voice, we ended up compromising that I needed a moderate amount of fixing, and that my wife could stand a bit of fixing too and the kids would hopefully fix themselves once we were fixed.

So as a matter of keeping the peace, I sat back down and spent the rest of our time with the group making fun of the all too pleasant group leader in my head and remaining skeptical about how much fixing I actually needed . . . and wishing that there was a faster, easier way to fix my kids.

22. THINGS THAT I REALLY HATE WHEN THEY HAPPEN

1. I accidentally end a phone call with my boss by saying "I love you," like I would to my wife.
2. I realize my zipper has been down, causing me to mentally retrace my steps to figure out when I left it down and how many people now think I'm a weirdo.
3. I realize the toilet paper roll is empty after it's too late, causing me to do that funny waddle to the cabinet where the toilet paper is kept. Which reminds me, I need to ask my wife, why it's necessary to keep the toilet paper in the hallway cabinet, instead of the one in the bathroom.
4. I put on my oven mitts and carefully take the casserole dish out of the oven, making sure not to let my arm touch the hot rack, put the dish on the hot pads that I have set out on the counter, take off the oven mitts . . . and then grab the four hundred degree lid with my bare hand.
5. There's always that one bottle of dressing that doesn't have a shaker-top. . . nothing like a bowl of ranch garnished with a little lettuce.
6. I realize after a loud and lengthy argument with my kids, that I was wrong and they were right about something. Especially after using terms like, "I've been around a little longer than you have" and "I wouldn't be arguing with you if I was wrong."

I sometimes, don't even bother telling them I was wrong. I'm sure that someone will tell my daughter that Japan is not the capital of China before she graduates, but I'm not. I won the argument fair and square. In the future, I need to remember to check Wikipedia BEFORE the argument.

23. I WANT MORE

I think it's in our nature as humans to wish we had more. I don't think that this is necessarily a bad thing as long as it doesn't reach the level of obsession or greed. Many great things that have been done in this world have started from a simple wanting of more. The Civil Rights movement was brought about by wanting more rights than what were given to minorities.

There are many things to pick from when considering what a person might want more of. More money would buy me more tacos, a new lawn mower and one of the Star Trek phasers that was actually used on the set during the filming of an episode. More money would mean that I had to work less, sometimes less is more. People can wish for more of all sorts of things. More peace in the world, more ambition to exercise, more opportunities, or more children (I shudder to even think).

But when I consider all of the things I could have more of, I always end up focusing on one particular thing. I wish I had more time. I'm not even sure I'm talking about more time being added on to the end of my life. I just need more time in the day.

Before I had children, it seemed like I had time, lots of time. I can even remember being bored when I was younger. Anymore, boredom would be a blessing. There is always something 'now' that needs to be done. There is almost never a moment when I'm not running a daughter here or there or trying to catch up on fixing the house and doing yard work so that the neighbor kids will stop referring to us as "the crazy people who live in the haunted house."

I want more time to be the dad that I am in my head. I want to be a dad who has time to play catch, and help with homework, and have long meaningful discussions with his kids. It's like my girls are stealing all my time but leaving me no time to spend with my girls.

Any time I do take to go fishing, play Xbox, or work on one of my inventions like the walk-in microwave, just leaves me feeling guilty. I feel like I shouldn't be wasting the time, and it robs me of any of the fun I was hoping it would produce.

If I could have more of something, time is definitely what I would want. I need a 36 hour day. Maybe I'll get more time when I'm retired. Of course, if I did find myself with more time once I'm retired, I'll probably end up wishing I had more money . . . or more time with my children and the grandchildren who will be stealing their time.

24. CHRISTMAS SHOPPING

The wife and I are Christmas shopping at the mall. It would be tough for me to choose between Christmas shopping at the mall and being dragged through a parking lot on my back, in my underwear, by a chain hooked to a bulldozer while the Mormon Tabernacle Choir repeatedly shot me with BB guns.

Unfortunately I wasn't given the choice. So here I am, wandering for hours around a crowded mall full of Christmas shopping psychopaths, trying in vain to find just one of the presents on the lists we were given. Hoping in vain that at least a few of the list items are in stock, the right color, the right version, and costing less than two of my paychecks. I call it mission impossible.

But it doesn't help that it gets so much harder to Christmas shop as the kids get older. They used to entertain themselves for days with the boxes the gifts came in. They didn't care that the gift itself was an outfit and benefitted the recipient's mother more than the child. They were just happy to rip off wrapping paper.

And then they get a little older, and you actually have to start putting some thought into their Christmas bounty. But it still wasn't too difficult to get a "This is the best Christmas ever!" out of them. You simply picked a few toys that were remotely close to what you'd seen them playing with at their friends' houses and you were a hero.

Then they become teenagers, and Christmas shopping becomes a source of great anxiety. The joy that was once a part of buying and giving gifts to our girls now sounds more like this:

"This is the 4.0 version, I wanted the 4.1."

"These aren't real Uggs, I'd just rather not have boots."

"It's fine, I said I liked it, now leave me alone."

"That's all I get this year?"

"I told you I just wanted money."

"Why is hers blue, you know I like blue, not red."

"Do I have to stay here all day or can I go over to Christy's house? We already unwrapped our presents."

My vote is to just give them money and call it good. But my wife still likes to try and make their Christmas special. Although the shopping is annoying, I love her for trying. Someday, probably when my daughters are disappointing their own kids on Christmas morning, maybe for just a brief moment they will think back and appreciate the time and money their mother and I are spending in this nightmarish mall shopping trip.

25. T'WAS THE NIGHT BEFORE CHRISTMAS.

T'was the night before Christmas, and all through our home,
   The children kept stirring, and making dad groan.

The stockings were still, in the boxes downstairs,
   No presents were wrapped, dad's pulling his hair.

The children were hyper, and out of their heads,
   And simply refused to go to their beds.

Though mom did her best at calming down dad,
   The later it got, the more he got mad.

Then with a loud crash, of his fist on the wall,
   Dad screamed "GO TO BED, OR NO PRESENTS AT ALL!"

Kids ran from the living room, and started to scatter,
   In fear that their butt cheeks, might soon be in tatters.

Away to their bedrooms, they flew like a flash,
   And then off went mom, to get the toy stash.

Til midnight they wrapped, sipped glasses of wine,
   And grumbled that bedtime, had not been at nine.

Jon Ziegler

More angry dad got, as hours ticked by,
Mom's patience was spent, she started to cry.

At last they were done, all presents were wrapped,
They might not be perfect, but who gives a crap.

Two hours of sleep, is all they would get,
Til on their bed jumped, the children and pets.

Complaining they rose, and went down to the tree,
And watched presents unwrap, kids squealing in glee.

All the money and time, the night without rest
was worth all the fuss to make this day best.

26. ABSENT MINDEDNESS

It is no secret amongst people who know me that I can tend to be a bit absent minded. I'm not sure if it's a matter of just being forgetful, or more a matter of my mind wandering causing me to forget to remember things in the first place. Or more than likely, it's a combination of the both. Being an absent-minded dad has its advantages and disadvantages.

One advantage is I tend to forget things that I probably should worry about. So I often deal with a lot less stress than some other parents. It is not uncommon for people I come into contact with to say something like, "So how is that situation with Natalie going? I know it has had the both of you pretty worried."

This usually is followed by me simultaneously answering "Ummm, it's going ok . . ." All the while I search my brain frantically for what it is about Natalie that I should be concerned about.

Later, when I ask my wife what it is that is supposed to have us concerned about Natalie, I would get an answer something like, "Did you forget she has bitten four kids in her class and the teacher this week?"

I would, of course, then remember the biting incidents and realize that I had not worried about it as much as maybe I should have because none of the victims had reported needing stitches. So things such as my darling youngest child biting students and teachers tend to cause a lot less stress for me than perhaps the average parent.

But then I'm always reminded of the disadvantages as well. A few days ago, I had to drop off a book that my older daughter, Hannah, had forgotten to take to school. Feeling like a responsible, caring parent, I proudly marched into the school's office and asked the secretary if she could make sure the book would get to my daughter.

"What grade is she in?" she asked.

"Ummm . . . I'm not sure," I said a little embarrassed.

"Well, how old is she?"

I was even more embarrassed that I couldn't remember how old my daughter was. "Uhhh . . . she's about this tall," I answered, holding up my hand.

The secretary looked at me with a look of bewilderment.

I was, however, able to provide her with my daughter's name.

27. DINNER

As I have mentioned before, my wife often works long hours at the hospital, leaving me in charge of creating some sort of dinner on many nights. The process of thinking up, shopping for, and implementing such meals seems to get more and more complicated every year. It ends up becoming a full-time job.

"What do you do for a living?"

"I make dinner for four people."

Little does the person asking this question know what all this involves when it comes to our family. There are certain guidelines that must be followed in order to appease all partakers of each meal.

Hannah likes Italian or Mexican, but not in the same week, and not either two days in a row. This presents a problem that is mathematically unsolvable.

Natalie is less concerned with the ethnic origin of a meal, but doesn't like food that is "green stuff covered in red," smells like cat fur (?), feels like socks in her mouth (?), or has the word "roasted" in the name.

My wife, after a visit to a more naturally oriented doctor, has been put on a gluten-free, dairy-free, low-carb diet.

Out of the five hundred page cook book that was given to me by my mother, these meal restrictions eliminate ninety-seven percent of the recipes right off the bat. Of the remaining few recipes, I still have to put them through the

Natalie test of trying to determine if they feel like socks in the mouth or smell like cat fur, two requirements that I do not even know precisely what they mean. By the time I figure out a dish that fits all the above requirements, it is almost guaranteed that I, myself, will find the resulting meal repulsive.

My attempts at getting input from the other three on what they DO want to have for dinner usually ends up producing no suggestions at all.

"I'm trying to make up the dinner menu, are there any suggestions?"

"Not Mexican or Italian, we already had those this week."

"Ok, then what do you like?"

"I like Mexican or Italian, just not any more this week."

"Natalie? Do you have any suggestions?"

"Nothing that feels like a sock . . . or was once alive." (The 'nothing that was once alive' was a completely new restriction that complicated things even further.)

"Ummmm, well I guess that leaves salt, you can eat salt for dinner. It was never alive."

"No, salt smells like cat fur."

My wife is the least picky of the group as far as taste, but her doctor prescribed diet made her just as hard to cook for as the other two lunatics.

Once I had spent several hours researching and questioning the eaters, I was finally able to settle on spaghetti for one meal, which I was able to sell as Italian-American to pacify Hannah. And although technically the ingredients had once been alive, I pointed out that spaghetti had never actually walked around and pooped like an animal to pacify Natalie, and a separate preparation of rather disgusting looking gluten-free pasta for my wife.

Now comes the task of preparing the agreed upon meal, which can involve making as many as three versions of the same dish. The spaghetti making could be accomplished with the making of one sauce with ground beef for Hannah, my wife and I, one sauce meatless to satisfy Natalie's aversion to eating things that have walked around pooping, one pan of normal gluten laden noodles, and one pan of gluten free pasta.

While I am cooking, I am faced with the constant chorus of both girls asking when dinner would be ready, why it was so late, am I sure that tomato sauce wasn't the blood from something that walked around and pooped? Also, my wife is constantly making sure that there is no gluten cross contamination occurring by using the same pans and spoons to cook the separate versions of the decided upon meal.

Finally, at eight o'clock, our dinner had been decided upon and cooked. It was now time to start the night's argument between my wife and daughters over whether they had to sit and eat at the table like a "normal family," or be allowed to wander and graze about the living room with the TV on and iPods playing in their ears.

This is normally where my wife looks to me for back up to enforce her "sit at the table dogma," but I am too exhausted from the three hours of researching, negotiating and preparing the several versions of the meal. All I can offer is a muffled "Uhgrumph!" as I shovel in a fork of spaghetti while it is still hot.

It takes another forty-five minutes of debate and moving myself and plate of food from the living room to the dining room table and finally back to the living room to finish my dinner.

Now that the meal-argument-tantrum has finally been completed by all, a second argument over clearing the table and putting the dishes in the dishwasher begins. Each night, either my wife or I will engage the girls in an attempt to make them "more responsible" and to "do their part around the house" by trying to get them to perform the meal clean up. On some nights, one of us will have the energy and feistiness to follow through with the arguments and threats required to get the girls to perform the table clearing and dish duties. But often, I find it to be much less effort on my part to just do it myself and save all the hassle.

So threatening to outlaw the use of dishes(by making everyone grab a handful of dinner out of the pan it was cooked in and take it into the bathroom to stand and eat it over the bathtub), I clear the table and load the dishwasher.

Finally, at ten o'clock, I am able to sit down and relax knowing that I had survived the creation of yet another meal and that no one in the house would starve to death for at least another day.

But already, the dread of tomorrow's dinner is looming in the back of my mind.

28. WHAT GUYS DO TOGETHER

Guys like to hang out in garages and pole barns, even though their wives "don't understand why anyone would want to just hang out in a garage or pole barn!" But then, that's partly why guys like to hang out in garages or pole barns.

Guys like to work on things like their cars or other handyman projects together. It's often more about the doing than the accomplishing. There is a comradery built between two guys who are not mechanics figuring out how to change a ball joint or drive shaft. There is a great victory in completing such projects, even if it took longer and cost more money than to having a professional do it.

Guys like to talk about the good old days before they had to be respectable and make mortgage and car payments. They like to make it sound like all the 'wild and crazy' things they used to do, were much wilder and crazier than what every other guy used to do. It seems to comfort them in the fact that they had to settle down and become respectable.

Guys like to complain about their wives and children. They huff and say things like, "I'm putting my foot down!" or "I'm not gonna take it anymore!" Guys like to make it sound as if they are the only reasonable person residing within their household. But in reality, if they really had to admit the truth of the situation, they would be completely lost without their wives and kids.

29. HOW TO MAKE A DAD MAD

*Turn off the shower when you have finished, but don't turn the knob with the arrow on it that switches the water from coming out of the shower head, to flowing out the spout. So when dad goes to turn on the water, (which requires that he bends over, placing his head directly in the crosshairs of the shower head) he is blasted full force in the face with freezing cold water for the ten seconds it takes to swear and find the knob with the arrow on it that switches the water from the shower to the spout.

*Call his favorite band or song a "classic" or an "oldie."

*In the middle of a heated lecture on not taking care of your messes in the living room and kitchen, point out that his bowl that he used for his fruity pebbles is still sitting on the coffee table from that morning.
   But be cautious. He will turn red and sputter for a few seconds, after which, you should probably be out of arms reach.

*Let him discover that the source of a seemingly endless supply of fruit flies in the house, are coming from a bowl of some unidentifiable organic matter under your bed.

*Drag him around on a six hour shopping trip that covers thirteen different stores, and then a return visit to eight of them, in an attempt to find a pair of shoes like Emily has, only to return to the very first store we looked in and decide to purchase the very first pair of shoes you tried on. And then, for the bonus dose of fury, tell him the following day that you don't like them and refuse to wear them.

*Don't answer the phone when he calls and then tell him your ringer was off, even though he could see you through the glass doors of the school entrance when you pulled the phone out of your pocket and looked at it when it rang.

*In the middle of a heated argument about why your grades are so low, say something like, "maybe I'm just not the kind of person who gets good grades. Why can't you just accept me for who I am?"
Even though your teachers and placement tests indicate you are capable of performing at an above average level.

*Leave the screen door standing wide open while you talk to someone outside during the middle of mosquito season instead of talking through the screen provided.

*Tell everyone that you caught him tearing up at the end of Bambi the last time the both of you watched the DVD.

*Spend the change from buying a movie ticket with the fifty dollar bill he gave you because he didn't actually say he wanted the change.

30. PARENTS AND TECHNOLOGY

My daughter is stuck at home tonight with two parents who are not only technically challenged, but who also just switched from Androids to iPhones. She has had an iPhone for a year now. The conversation sounds a bit like this:

"Why is there no back button? My Android had a back button."

"How do I sync my email?"

"Just a minute, I'm helping mom make the screen letters bigger."

"You've been helping her for a half hour, it's my turn. Where the heck is the internet?"

"It's called Safari"

"Leave her alone she's helping me"

"SAFARI? That's stupid."

For the first twenty minutes, she seems somewhat pleased that WE, the parents, are so dependent upon her to perform even the most basic of functions on our new smart phones. But as the night wears on, she becomes less amused at our ignorance.

"Where's my contacts list? Why isn't it right down here at the bottom like my other phone?"

"DAD, I've told you four times how to get to your contacts list! It hasn't changed since that last time five minutes ago!"

"How do I get my songs on here from iTunes?"

"I want to turn my picture into a zombie like you did the other day. What was that app called?'

"Why does it keep saying that I need an Apple ID? That's stupid!"

Unfortunately, all across the globe, scenarios like this are being played out in living rooms, night after night.

Like my wife and I, many parents our age did not grow up in a digital, computer dependent world full of smart phones, email addresses, and WIFI. These are all things we have had to learn and to adapt too. At times, our analog, pencil and paper geared minds can get overloaded. A new smart phone can be horrifying as opposed to the excitement my daughters would feel. I just barely learned how to operate all the functions on my old phone, and now you want me to throw it all out and start from scratch?

In our day, if you learned how to use the U.S. Postal Service, you could reasonably expect that the skill would carry you through the rest of your life without needing to alter how you use the Mail system's OS (operating system, I just learned that one from my daughter). If you learned how to look up a number in the phone book and dial the telephone that hung on the wall, you were pretty much set. But then all this new stuff comes along and ruins everything.

Kids nowadays were born into this cyber world, and their brains are trained to think that way from day one. They adapt to changes in technology and operating systems so much faster than I can.

Gone are the days when a father could proudly teach his son or daughter the simple life skills they needed to be able to interact with the world around them. Most of the technical learning that goes on in our household is daughter teaching parent.

We recently switched from cable TV to satellite TV. This change required that I learn a whole new OS. This change was a creator of much stress for me. I felt like a turtle on my back. I couldn't make a TV show even appear on the screen, let alone one I wanted to watch.

But I have learned to cope with my technological disabilities, and overcome them. When the new satellite box was fired up for the first time and I had spent the ten minutes required to determine that I had no idea how to operate it, I simply handed the remote to my daughter Hannah and left the room. This is known as step one.

After an hour I returned, and just as I suspected, she had mastered the system. She could perform any and every function available. In fact, she had already set up her own channel favorites list and had set the DVR that came with it to record her shows.

Step two is to have Hannah simply show me how to turn the channel box on and off.

Step three is an on-going step. Step three is to use Hannah like a voice controlled remote for the next month or two as I slowly learn each satellite TV skill one at a time.

"Hannah, make it go to The Discovery Channel."

"Hannah, make it record Wildest Police Video episodes."

"Hannah, make Netflix come up on the screen."

This system has helped to eliminate much of the anxiety and fear that can be the result of trying to learn a new technology or OS. I'd like to think that over time, my ability to adapt to such changes would become easier and easier. But I'm beginning to realize that all the gains I make as far as becoming fluent in the computer-digital-cyber world, are being countered by my memory becoming duller, and perhaps a touch of senility setting in.

31. THE HEARING PROBLEMS OF DAUGHTERS

My daughters don't seem to hear things within the same realm or reality that I do. Somehow, what I say is ultimately not what they end up hearing. I can't figure out if there is a physical problem with their hearing, a mental problem such as schizophrenia that needs to be addressed or they are simply trying make me look as bad as possible in front of their mom. Perhaps it is simply a bad case of the dramas.

For example, when my girls were ages ten and twelve, they both decided to join the local softball league together. I'm not the biggest sports fan, but I was excited that the girls wanted to get involved with something other than watching TV, so I was more than willing to purchase gloves, balls and bats in order for them to be able to practice.

I am also not the most skilled at any particular sport, but I can throw, catch and pitch well enough to help my rookie daughters get used to playing. One night after work, I eagerly took them outside to begin some practice on basic softball skills.

For nearly two hours, we played catch and practiced batting. Both girls, who had never played before, actually did quite well for beginners, but their lack of experience left much room for improvement.

At the end of our practice session, I said in my coach-like voice, "That was good girls. With a little more practice, I think you will both make fine softball players!"

Hannah threw her glove on the ground and stomped into the house crying loudly. Natalie stood silently looking at me with large tear-filled, puppy dog eyes for a moment, and then followed suit. Puzzled, I picked up the pile of gloves, balls and bat, and put them in the shed.

Upon entering the house, my wife confronted me, "Why would you say that to them? They are just learning to play."

"SAY WHAT?" I plead, "I told them they did very well and that they would make good players with a little more practice!"

My wife gave me a look of skepticism, "Natalie said that you told them that they were the worst players EVER, and that they needed A LOT of practice if they didn't want to get kicked off the team. Hannah says you made fun of them and she is never going to play again."

Such was my introduction to the mind of a teenage daughter and how it works. I now know that what I say, and what is heard, can be two completely different things.

If I say, "Clean your room or there will be consequences!" my daughter's interpretation will be, "Dad said if we don't clean our room, he will punch us in the face and throw us out of the house to live in boxes like the people who live on the sidewalk in Detroit."

Or if they ask me if they can go spend the night with a friend next weekend, I might answer, "Maybe, we'll see". But then if it doesn't work out for whatever reason, they are sure to cry bloody murder, "DAD PROMISED ME THAT I COULD SPEND THE NIGHT AT CHRISTY'S HOUSE THIS WEEKEND AND NOW HE'S GOING BACK ON HIS WORD."

And then sometimes, they don't hear what I say at all. It's as if I don't even exist! I can be sitting across the dining room table from one of them, and say in a loud, clear voice, "Stop spitting your vegetables onto your plate."

They will look me straight in the eyes, and spit out another wad of broccoli, as if the words not to spit out your vegetables had never left my mouth.

How can they hear more than what I actually say sometimes, and then not hear a thing that I say at other times?

Maybe I should take them to see a doct-. . . Now that I'm thinking about it, I have similar problems when communicating with my wife. Last week, I was wearing my favorite Star Trek T-shirt that has a few character holes and stains on it.

"I think it's time you stopped wearing that shirt in public," she commented.

I simply gave her a blank look without saying a word to avoid an argument.

Yesterday, when I was again wearing my favorite Star Trek shirt, she declared in a tone of irritation, "I thought we agreed that we wouldn't wear that shirt in public anymore."

Just as was the case with my daughters, she apparently remembers a conversation that never took place. She had simply stated her desire for me to stop wearing the shirt. I hadn't responded at all. There had been no conversation, and certainly no agreement.

I began to worry that it was me. Maybe I was only remembering half of the things I said. Or not remembering conversations at all! To satisfy my curiosity, I began carrying around a small tape recorder and recording conversations. I would then play them back whenever I noticed any discrepancies in how my words were recounted to me by a daughter or my wife. Just as I had suspected, the recordings were testament to my not saying everything I was accused of.

So now, instead of expressing things verbally, I carry around a notebook. Whenever I say something like, "Maybe you can spend the night at Christy's on Saturday," I write it down and have the daughter at which the comment was directed sign and date it.

This has alleviated some of the disputes, but doesn't help much with conversations that never took place. The only answer to that problem, that I can figure, is to have each member of the household sign an affidavit every ten minutes that states no conversation had taken place in the prior time period.

32. MY WIFE HAS MY BACK

I opened my eyes to a world of confusion. I could tell from my grogginess, that I must have been sleeping very soundly. I wasn't even sure that I wasn't still sleeping and dreaming.

Before me was my wife, sitting with a red face, and looking at me with a horrified expression. As my vision and mind cleared a little, I realized that I was standing in the sanctuary of our church. My wife was not the only one with a look of terror on her face. The whole congregation was there . . . staring at me . . . with looks on their faces like I was evil incarnate. Still not sure whether I was dreaming or not, I took my seat in the pew next to my wife, who was still staring at me with her mouth open.

After a few awkward moments of silence and glaring looks, the minister began speaking a sermon that I had obviously not heard the first part of.

"WHAT WAS THAT?" my wife said in a whisper that sounded more like a yell.

"What was what?" I asked as I began to have recollections of it being Sunday.

"Who is Gerald??" she said, still obviously quite agitated.

I shrugged, having no clue what she was talking about.

It looked like she was about to start yelling, when she suddenly stopped and grabbed a piece of paper and a pen from her purse. She then began to write large angry words with so much pressure on the paper, that the sound was getting the attention of the people around us. When she had finished, she handed it to me with disgust.

It said, "You were sleeping and snoring in the middle of the service! When I tried to wake you up, you jumped up and screamed "GERALD!! JUST HIT THAT LLAMA IN THE HEAD WITH THE SHOVEL, YOU DUMBA&&!!!"

When she could tell I had finished reading the note, she crinkled it up and threw it at me, hitting me in the forehead.

As the reality of what had just transpired began to sink in, I felt the redness of embarrassment rush to my face. I did my best to slouch down in the pew and become invisible for the rest of the service. I was sure that at the very moment I had yelled the word "dumba&&" in church, I had contracted some form of terminal cancer.

At long last, the service ended. I exited the sanctuary as fast as I could without making it obvious that I was running and headed straight for our car in the parking lot.

I knew that I had an intense lecture coming from my mortally embarrassed wife, but to her credit I knew that she remained in the church longer than usual in order to explain away my ridiculous actions. I imagined that she was probably employing her knowledge as a nurse to convince the other members of the congregation that I had contracted Tourette's.

She has come to my rescue for similar situations many times throughout our marriage. She has become a master of easing the embarrassment and anger caused by my sometime impulsive and irrational behavior, and for that I am truly grateful.

Being a nurse, she has been able to utilize her knowledge of the many different psychological and physiological conditions that can cause a person to act in an embarrassing way, such as her blaming my unholy outburst on Tourette's.

Another condition she relies on when attempting to explain away my actions is to claim that when my sugar gets low, it makes me do crazy things. This particular excuse was used at a family funeral where I had become convinced that my uncle Leon was faking his own death as a joke, and then found out otherwise but only after I had drawn a magic-marker a mustache on his face and set his necktie on fire as he lay in his casket.

It would seem that the torch of covering for my ill-planned actions has been passed on to my daughters as well. They have become masters of justifying my antics to avoid being humiliated in front of their friends. Hannah once told her classmates that part of my hair had been burned off while rescuing a litter of puppies from a burning building, rather than telling them that I had actually shaved off half of my hair due to being convinced that I had contracted lice only on the left side of my head.

It is actually a bit comforting to know that my family is so eager to stand behind me no matter what I end up doing. But I do sometimes feel a bit of regret that their defense of my actions is often born out of their own embarrassment. None the less, I am truly grateful for my wife and daughters. There is likely few other people on this earth who would put up with me.

33. GLIMPSES OF LIGHT

Sometimes, the world of a parent who truly loves a child with all their heart is a world of fretting, sleepless nights and constant analyzing of "where are my children's lives heading?"

If it's a battle to get them to pick up after themselves or clean their rooms, I set my prediction of their life course to end at them being one of those hoarders on TV. I fear they will live in houses that you can't walk through. I envision newspapers and piles of dirty clothes stacked to the ceiling, and rotting food in dishes making it impossible to breathe.

If they get into trouble at school because of a fight, I perceive that they are headed for a life of violence, probably joining a gang and spending Friday nights performing drive-by shootings and fire-bombings, ending in them spending the rest of their lives in prison.

I understand that I may be letting my imagination get a little out of control, but it is only because I want them to grow into young adults that I can be proud of. I want them to accomplish even more than I have been able to accomplish. I don't want to be one of those parents who ignored the signs of trouble and end up wondering what went wrong only after their kids' lives have spun out of control.

But then there are those little glimpses of light that poke through all the arguing, eye rolling, and frustration that might suggest, your kids may actually be turning out the way you had hoped. It might be something as simple as picking up dirty clothes without you having to scream at them. Or an act of kindness that shows they do have consideration for people other than themselves. They might have actually heard something in one of the many character building lectures that has stayed with them. Or maybe these moments of light had nothing to do with my lectures; maybe they are developing awesome personalities in spite of my parenting.

But whatever it is that causes these positive traits to begin developing within them, it gives a paranoid father a little hope that he might actually be doing something right, or at the very least, isn't doing everything wrong.

It is these little glimpses of light poking through that are the moments that make it all worth it.

34. THE WORST BEST ANNIVERSARY EVER

Every year, stuck in between thanksgiving and Christmas is mine and my wife's anniversary. And every year, due to the mayhem created by coordinating our attendance at two separate family Thanksgivings, and three different Christmases all occurring on different weekends, I forget that it is our anniversary until we are well into the day itself.

But this year was going to be different. This year I would be ready to give her the best anniversary ever.

On the day of our anniversary, I had arranged to deliver the girls to aunts and uncles houses for the night, leaving my wife and I free to enjoy the evening without the complications of two daughters. And I made sure to have them delivered in time to make it back home before my wife arrived.

With much anticipation, I sat on the couch and waited for my wife to get home from work. I was very excited about the romantic night I had been planning for over a week now.

Upon her arrival, I led my anniversary girl into the living room, where she was greeted by our cat Cee Cee dressed in a top hat and bow tie, and our dog Pippi who was wearing my wife's wedding dress.

"What the heck? Why is the stinky dog wearing my . . ."

"I knew you would say that, so I put deodorant on her armpits so that she wouldn't make your dress smell like a dog," I quickly replied, and then clapped my hands to signal the start of the recreation of our wedding that I had rehearsed with both animals all week.

Cee Cee sat silently purring, and Pippi licked at her armpits where I had applied the deodorant. Neither seemed to remember the roles we had practiced.

My wife looked at me with a frown, presumably due to Pippi wearing her wedding dress that had to be altered with duct tape and safety pins to fit her.

"Just wait," I said nervously and clapped my hands again.

Cee Cee remained motionless. Pippi licked her armpit one more time, and then threw up on the wedding dress train.

"Dang it!" My wife yelled, snatching the dress from off of the dog and taking it to the bathroom to run it under water.

"I'm sorry, dear, I didn't know that the deodorant would make her throw up," I offered pathetically.

"Grrrrrrrrr," my wife grumbled and hung the still vomit stained dress on a hanger.

"Well, never mind the wedding recreation, let's just open your gift!" I announced to shift her attention.

Taking her by the hand and leading her to the couch, I sat her down and presented her with my gift of love.

"I was thinking that we need to spend more fun time together, so this gift is something that we can both do as a happily married couple."

Just then, my wife finished tearing off the last of the Star Wars wrapping paper to reveal her brand new . . . fishing pole.

At first she stared blankly at the Shimano bait casting reel mounted on an eight foot medium to heavy duty rod (a fishing pole I had wanted for myself for quite a while now), and then shifted her glance to me.

"Oh, it's a joke, right?" She said, giving a fake laugh.

"You don't like it?"

Realizing that it may not have been a joke, she sighed and said, "You know I don't like to go fishing."

"Well yes, but I thought you might like it more if we were doing it as a happily married couple . . ."

With a forced politeness, she set the pole down and went into the bathroom. Feeling as if I had just been given my second strike, I followed her to the bathroom door and knocked on it lightly.

"Well, if you don't like it, do you mind if I use it?"

There was no answer.

Once again, I decided it best to change the subject.

"Ok, never mind all that, I've made us reservations at my fav-. . . I mean, OUR favorite restaurant, Ray's Taco Palace!"

I wasn't sure, but I thought I could hear a groan from within the bathroom.

So with the first two disasters behind us, we headed off for the delightful Mexican cuisine that awaited us at Ray's.

At the restaurant, I had made special arrangements with the owner, who was named Ray, to have a candle lit table and his Somalian dishwasher, Hassan, serenade us in an odd mix of broken English and broken Spanish while we ate. Finally, we could begin a romantic anniversary evening together.

We chatted pleasantly together about getting the wedding dress dry cleaned and how great my wife's new fishing pole would be when I borrowed it for my next fishing trip until the waiter finally arrived with our orders.

"This is going to be great!" I squealed as my favorite dish, Ray's heaping plate of garlic beans and onions, was set down before me. But again, I caught my wife giving me the now familiar look of disapproval as I began to lap it down like a starving dog. I assumed that she was probably angry at not ordering the garlic beans for herself when the potent smell clued her into how good it actually was. None the less, I was in Mexican heaven, sitting across from the woman I loved, anxious to get her home where a childless house and a night of romance awaited.

Finally, the plate of beans had been devoured and Hassan was just finishing a tear-jerking rendition of "Love Me Afectuoso (tender)." So we thanked Ray for the wonderful dinner and headed out to our car.

Once we were finally at home, and alone, I dimmed the lights and joined my beautiful wife on the couch with two glasses of Champaign. Then, leaning in close and looking her straight in the eyes, I said, "I truly love you and I am so glad that we are married."

For a second, she closed her eyes and wrinkled up her nose, making me think that she was fighting back tears. She leaned back and drew in a breath and then began to heave as if she were going to throw up.

"I'm sorry, but your breath is making me sick. You smell like garlic and onions and, and, did you fart?"

Giving my breath the hand to mouth sniff test, I was surprised at just how bad my breath did stink. And I was embarrassed to admit, "Welllll, I might have let a small one out. But I couldn't help it! The beans have me all torn up! I didn't think you would notice one that small!"

Standing up from the couch, my wife chugged the glass of Champaign, and set the glass down on the coffee table. Then, stopping only to throw a blanket and pillow at me on the couch, she started walking towards the stairs.

"WAIT, WAIT! I'll brush my teeth! I'll gargle!" I pleaded standing to follow behind her. But suddenly, I realized that I needed to be in the bathroom and sitting on the toilet immediately. So I ran, passing my wife in the dining room before she could reach the stairs and slamming the bathroom door shut behind me.

After a ten minute bathroom session that could only be described as "life changing," I returned to the living room where I spent the remainder of the evening wallowing in my own stench and making the occasional trip to the toilet. I found myself sleeping alone on the couch except for our dog Pippi's who was attempting to roll in me as if I were a smelly dead animal.

As a consolation, I did receive a text from my wife that read, "I love you and I truly appreciate the amount of effort you put into our anniversary, but maybe I won't be so angry if you happen to forget it next year :)."

35. RULE WITHOUT REASON

In our house, there are many rules. Such as, no leaving dirty laundry on the bathroom floor, no feeding the dog human food, no TV before homework, no trying to unclog the toilet with kitchen utensils . . ., etc.

Most of these rules were put in place for a reason, and serve to ensure that things do not get out of control, or that past disasters are not repeated. I have no problem with these rules. However, there are a small percentage of rules that seem to have no logical reason behind them. For example: you must make your bed each morning or no cleaning and scaling fish in the kitchen sink.

One such nonsensical rule states that no hats shall be worn at the dinner table. And being a baseball hat wearer, this rule has been the cause of many fights in our house. Almost daily, when dinner is served, I arrive and sit down at the table with my hat on. I am then told to remove it before starting to eat. At this point, I have to decide whether I am too tired or hungry to engage in the ongoing argument about why I can't wear a hat to the table.

To date, the only reason I have been able to get out of the dinner rule enforcer (my wife) is that we don't wear hats at the table because that's the way it's always been.

I once spent an entire week preparing a well thought out presentation that included charts, legal citing's, and a report from my doctor that stated hat wearing had no negative effects on digestion, but to no avail. My presentation fell on deaf ears.

For a while, I was looking into converting to Judaism, so that I could claim religious persecution if she tried to get me to remove my Yarmulke (a baseball hat without the bill) for dinner. But when I realized that becoming Jewish meant that I had to give up bacon and pork rinds, I decided it wasn't worth it just to be able to wear a hat to dinner.

But I'm not one to just give in so easily, especially when it comes to basic civil rights issues. I found a tiny little baseball hat that belonged to one of my daughter's Lego people that was about the size of a pea. And with some effort, I've found that I have just enough hair left on top of my head, that I can hide the tiny hat in it with the aid of a bobby pin. So now, when I'm told to remove my full sized "decoy" hat, I am secretly still wearing the little Lego hat.

Even though she is not even aware of my secret protest and I would still much rather be wearing my full sized hat, I get great satisfaction in knowing that I'm enjoying my meal with a hat on my head . . . I think it even makes the food taste better.

36. HAS THIS EVER HAPPENED TO YOU?

Have you ever been at a party where you didn't know a whole lot of people, and in the middle of the party, you realize that you really, really had to go to the bathroom, but not the kind of go to the bathroom that men can do standing up, rather the kind of going to the bathroom that even men have to do sitting down, but when you had finished, you realized that there was no toilet paper on the roll, but you are way too embarrassed to try yelling, "WILL SOMEBODY GET ME A ROLL OF TOILET PAPER?" so you waddle over to the shelves on the other side of the bathroom to search in vain for another roll of toilet paper, but after an extensive search, performed with your pants and underwear around your ankles like manacles, you finally realize that there is not a roll of toilet paper anywhere to be found, so you try calling the cell phone of the person who's house the party is being held at, but you only get their voicemail, so you leave them a very long and colorfully worded dissertation about making sure there is toilet paper in the bathroom before having a party, and then you go rummaging back through the cabinets with your pants and underwear still around your ankles, only to find the only suitable toilet paper substitute is a huge bag of Q-Tips?

It's never happened to me either. But if it had happened to me, I could assure you that it takes a whole lot of time and Q-Tips to finish your business.

37. NAVIGATING PARENTS

I'm always amazed at how quickly children are able to adapt and learn how to capitalize on situations. For instance, a child learns even before they learn to talk, that crying gets them attention, and often what they want. It is from this very basic concept, that children will build and perfect a method of parent manipulation. This perfecting of such methods continues throughout their childhood until they become masters at what I call "navigating parents."

Parent navigating involves knowing from past experience, which parent is best suited for each and every situation, whether it be confessing to wrong doing or soliciting something the child desires. And beyond even knowing which parent is the appropriate choice, they quickly learn what to say and how to act in order to maximize their chances at achieving the desired end result.

My daughter Natalie knew that my wife was the one to approach about purchasing a dress for her upcoming prom. In fact, she not only knew that my wife was the one to approach, but that the approach should be made without my knowledge. I guess I can't say that I blame her. I can only imagine how the conversation would have gone if it had been me she had solicited for the dress:

Child: "Dad, I need a dress for prom."

Me: "What's wrong with the hundred dresses in your closet?"

Child: "Those aren't prom dresses, and besides, nobody wears a dress to prom that isn't new."

Me: "What makes a dress a prom dress?"

Child: "It has to be stylish and sparkly."

Me: "A dress is a lot like a curtain. Mom has a lot of spare curtains in the closet. Why can't we just make a dress out of an old set of curtains and then attach sparkly things on it with that kit I saw advertised on TV?"

Child: "DDAAAAADDDDD!!!!!"

Me: "Fine, how much is this new, sparkly dress going to cost?" (Although I have no idea how much a dress costs, I'm thinking that fifty dollars is the upper end of her answer. In fact, I'm thinking that if I allow her to spend fifty dollars, it will be quite generous on my part.)

Child: "I found one on the clearance rack for . . . (proud that she had found one on the clearance rack, I'm now thinking I'm going to get out of this only spending thirty to forty dollars) three hundred and sixty four dollars.

This is the point at which my mouth will drop open and my eyes roll in the most dramatic eye roll I can muster, followed by me bellowing, "I DON'T CARE IF YOU GO TO THE PROM IN YOUR HANNAH MONTANA PAJAMAS! I'M NOT SPENDING THREE HUNDRED DOLLARS ON A DRESS YOU WILL ONLY WEAR ONCE!!!!"

Apparently this whole scenario has gone through my daughters mind at some point as well, which is why she would never approach me about a prom dress. She knows that mom, who probably spent a ridiculous amount on her own prom dress, will be much more sympathetic to her wishes. In fact, she will not only get the dress for the child, but help her keep it a secret from me in order to spare her the long lecture on the impracticality of such a ridiculous purchase.

But then on the other hand, when Hannah wanted to have permission to skip school for a day so that she could go to an amusement park with a group of friends, she wisely chose to approach me instead of my wife, due to my having what my wife describes as an "irresponsibly free spirit." She knows that school skipping takes me back to my own childhood. And that if I did actually try to put up any resistance, she need only say something like, "I always hear you talk about the wild and crazy things you did while you were in school, and I want to have some of my own wild and crazy things like that to tell my own kids!"

Kids know too, that it is important to choose the right parent from the beginning. They have all at one time or another tried asking one parent, and after not getting the response they were hoping for, tried the other parent. I think they know that they will not get away with it in the end, but they figure it's better to get permission from the second parent, and get into trouble for asking twice, than to go ahead and do something after being told not to by the one parent.

But careful research and planning can give the child an idea on which parent would be the best prospect for approaching first; often eliminating the need to petition the second parent for the desired response.

Yet another part of parent navigation is the knowing just which parent is the better choice for confessing to different types of crimes:

Bad report card: tell dad, he barely graduated high school, mom graduated college with honors.

Broke one of dad's new inventions he is working on that you weren't supposed to touch: tell mom, she is annoyed that dad spends money on them in the first place.

Got in a fight at school: tell mom, if you lost the fight. Her mothering instincts will kick in and she will be more concerned with the injuries rather than the fact that you were in a fight. Besides, if dad finds out you lost a fight, he is more likely to drive you over to the other kid's house to try again.

However, if you won the fight, tell dad, explaining that you were merely sticking up for yourself and not backing down from a bully.

I'm assuming that this practice of parent navigation will continue on through the rest of their lives. I can just imagine them choosing the right parent to ask for a loan to pay their car insurance or rent. I guess it's not so hard to tolerate knowing that at some point, as my wife and I get older and begin to need help in our golden years, we will start employing a similar method to get what we want, known as the "daughter navigation".

38. ANNOYING TRENDS IN FASHION

I get so annoyed at trends in fashion, the sizing of pants in particular. Why must jean sizes continue to change?

When I was in my teens, if I bought a pair of jeans with a label that says they have a twenty- eight inch waist, they actually fit my twenty-eight inch waist.

As time went on, the jeans that I bought with a twenty-eight inch waist kept getting smaller and smaller. I found that I had to start buying jeans with a thirty inch waist to fit my twenty-eight inch waist.

Now, a few decades later, this trend in improper jeans sizing has continued. I'm looking at buying thirty-four inch jeans to fit my twenty-eight inch waist!!!! Is there no agency that governs the fashion industry to make sure that when they label a pair of pants as twenty-eight inch waist, that they will actually fit a twenty-eight inch waist??!!!

39. BEAR HUGS

I have heard other fathers and even a mother or two, remark about not being as affectionate with their children as they grew older. "They have outgrown it," or "it just becomes awkward".

I've noticed that fathers in particular often feel that too much affection or hugging of daughters is somehow improper as they get into their teen years. I guess if it starts to feel improper, there is nothing else you can do but to stop.

However, I do not subscribe to this notion of slowly creating a barrier between myself and my girls. I maul them with hugs every chance I get, like a big bear. It is not uncommon for an epic wrestling match to break out in our living room either. It had never occurred to me that I shouldn't.

I guess it might be different had my girls expressed annoyance or shown uneasiness about my attacks of affection, or my hugs of consolation when they are upset or hurt, but they don't. In fact, it is sometimes they who hug me or lean against me like a sofa cushion while watching TV together.

I hope that they never outgrow it, and I will do everything I can to prevent it. I don't care if they are forty years old, they will be subject to a spontaneous rib crushing hug and kiss from their dad. After all, they always have and always will be my baby girls.

40. FOUR NON-MORNING PEOPLE GETTING READY FOR SCHOOL AND WORK

The alarm clock is always loud and obnoxious. It makes certain that I wake up in a bad mood. I snooze it a half dozen times, but it always returns, making me even angrier.

Then, like every morning, I remember that I need to sprint to the bathroom or suffer a fifteen minute wait in the event my wife beats me there. I notice that my wife is not in the bed beside me. This is not a good sign.

I run downstairs to find the bathroom door closed. I really need to go to the bathroom.

I knock on the door, "are you almost done?"

Silence.

"ARE YOU ALMOST DONE? I really need to go!"

"I'll be out in a minute, I just got in here," came the voice from inside.

I let out a growl and begin swearing in my head.

"STOP SWEARING, I SAID I'LL BE OUT IN A MINUTE!"

Apparently I was swearing in my head loud enough that it could be heard coming out of my mouth.

Just then my oldest daughter Hannah appears at the bottom the stairs with an expression on her face much like what I would imagine Jack the Ripper would have on his face. She barges past me and begins knocking on the bathroom door.

This signals the official start to the morning battle.

"STOP KNOCKING, I SAID I'LL BE OUT!!!" My wife screamed from within the bathroom.

"THATS THE FIRST TIME I'VE KNOCKED" Hannah replied in a demonic voice.

I rolled my eyes and began swearing in my head again, only this time I made sure it stayed in my head.

The dog looked up at me, smiling and mocking me for my discomfort at not being able to use the bathroom.

"Shut up you stupid animal!"

"WHAT DID YOU JUST SAY?" demanded the bathroom voice.

My daughter chuckled.

The dog wagged its tail.

"I was talking to the dog."

With the flush of the toilet, the bathroom door burst open and my extremely angry wife stormed past my extremely angry self and my extremely angry daughter.

Hannah scurried into the bathroom and slammed the door.

"JERK!" I yelled.

The dog was smiling even bigger now.

I could hold it no longer, so I ran out the kitchen door to the backyard, and relieved myself behind our lilac bush, the only spot in our yard hidden from the windows of all of the neighbors.

Back inside the house, I wandered towards bathroom, once again, to see if it had become vacant, but the door was still closed and I could hear the sound of the shower running.

The dog had vanished, but there sat a pile of poop where he had been mocking and smiling at my discomfort just moments before.

Just then I heard a footstep on the stairs. I turned to see her Royal Highness, the morning princess of darkness, my youngest daughter descending with a particularly evil aura emanating from her.

No one in the family would be described as being all that pleasant in the morning, but my daughter Natalie gave new meaning to the term "not a morning person." She elevated it to the level of rabid pit bull. She could be so nasty, that even I try not to get in her way. She has been this way for as long as I could remember. So much so, that when she was four, I tried giving her a cup of black coffee to see if it would improve things like it does for adults, but to no avail. It only seemed to super-charge her wickedness.

Natalie's arrival meant that the battle was now entering its peak viciousness.

"Get out of the bathroom!"

"I'm not done!"

"Where's my hair straightener?"

"I have it and it's not yours, yours is the blue one."

"I HATE the blue one!"

"MOM, Natalie threw her hair straightener at me!"

"Tell your dad, I'm running late."

"DAAAAD, Natalie threw her hair straightener at me!"

"Tell your mom; I'm cleaning up dog poop!"

"JERK!"

"I HATE YOU AND I WISH YOU WEREN'T MY SISTER!"

I have been waiting for my turn in the bathroom for thirty-seven minutes now. My wife, angry over the girls' argument storms into the bathroom and slams the door. There are now three females in a bathroom not big enough for one person and they are all in a rage.

There is screaming and the loud crashing sounds of a scuffle.

Then the door bursts open, and the three of females stomp out, sobbing and muttering terrible things about the others.

At this point, I have given up on getting a turn in the bathroom and have already started heading out to my truck to wait for her highness, who I take to school each day.

"I'm heading to the truck, Natalie, hurry up or we will both be late."

"I can't find any clean socks."

"I thought it was decided that we would find clean socks the night before, so we don't have this problem anymore."

Natalie ignores me, so I continued out the door to my truck.

After fifteen minutes of honking, Natalie finally emerges sockless and we are finally able to leave.

The final results to the morning battle looked something like this:

Hannah got to shower, but sustained a burn to her forearm while deflecting a red hair straightener that was thrown by Natalie. The red hair straightener was damaged beyond repair from hitting the edge of the toilet bowl after deflecting off of Hannah's arm. Hannah's hair was not straightened because of the red hair straightener's demise and her lack of confidence in the viability of the blue hair straightener.

Natalie was the only female who was able to straighten her hair, but went to school sockless and with a ripped shirt that was the result of my wife trying to wrestle the hair dryer from her hands. Adding to her list of injuries was the fact that her iPhone was dead due to her losing the battle over the only working phone charger the night before.

My wife did not have time for a shower so she applied an extra dose of deodorant and body spray to compensate. Her hair was 'splash' washed in the kitchen sink, but not straightened.

I was never able to get a turn in the bathroom at all. Other than urinating in the backyard and gargling with a bottle of mouthwash that I keep in my truck for mornings when I don't get to use the bathroom, I was heading off to work in my original awakening condition.

All four of us were late to school and work. All four of us were in terrible moods and were convinced that we had been severely mistreated by the other three.

I would consider this to be an average morning. You don't even want to hear about a bad one.

41. I'LL TAKE HIM!

It's funny to think about how some of the things that you are so sure of when your children are young, can change so drastically as they get older. I guess not every lofty parental idea ends up being quite as practical as you might have hoped, or maybe, we just get weary as parents and look for an easier way out.

When my daughters were very young, I liked to make grand statements like, "My daughter's will not date until they are twenty-eight!"

Statements like these were made with all the conviction that nearly every dad has when making statements concerning his daughters and dating. I had constructed in my mind, a minimum list of requirements for potential boyfriends. Items on the list included things like: never gets in any trouble, is deathly afraid of what I'll do to him if he hurts my daughter, has absolutely no hormones, is being scouted by several professional sports teams and has several scholarship offers from ivy league schools where he will finish pursuing his doctorate.

I think it's only natural for a parent to have these aspirations of grandeur; after all, we want the very best for our sons and daughters and don't want to see them making mistakes that could affect the rest of their lives.

But then, as my girls grew older and entered high school, I began to see their different personalities developing. And with that added knowledge, it sometimes leads to my changing my expectations and ideas for what would happen with the rest of their lives.

With one of my daughters, I began to notice a pattern in many of the friends she chose. They were by no means bad kids, in fact, I liked them. They just always seemed to be a bit on the "wild side," always a bit free spirited . . . like I was. Adding to this observation was the fact that she had occasionally gotten herself into a little trouble at school.

I knew that one day, this pattern of free spirited friends and a slight tendency to get into trouble at school would come into play when she picked potential boyfriends. When I considered these factors and then magnified, exaggerated and followed the scenario to the worst imaginable end result, the possibilities frightened me to say the least. I pictured an endless parade of baggy panted "bad boys" who never had jobs becoming her boyfriends, ending in her choosing one who, although seemed quite intelligent and fun to be around, would end up marrying my daughter and moving into our basement for several decades of unemployment while he "cut" his rap album that would never get finished and would not make him a dime even if it did. The imaginary scenario always ends in me committing an act of violence against my rapping loser of a son-in-law, and him saying things like, "YOU JUST DON'T APPRECIATE ME AS AN ARTIST, DUDE!" while I pummeled him senseless in my basement.

So when the news reached me through various leaks in her "don't tell dad" network, that my now ninth grade daughter liked one of the boys in the neighborhood, I immediately went into "I'll kill him" mode. It didn't matter that he seemingly had no interest in my daughter; I just knew that as a dad, my duty was to annihilate any incoming threats.

But in an attempt to be fair and with much skepticism, I silently watched for the rest of the year, gathering intel on the object of my daughters crush, and waiting for either one of them to step out of line.

But in that year, I noticed two things. One: the boy, although friendly to my daughter, didn't seem to have any romantic interest in her. And two: no matter how hard I looked, I couldn't find any dirt on him. He did very well in his classes. I could find no instances of him being in trouble. He didn't have large piercings all over his face or a tattoo on his forehead that said, "You Mad Bro?" He was a bit shy and seemed polite and respectful to adults. As much as I hated to admit it, he seemed like a good kid.

And then one day while I was comparing this young man to the many imaginary boyfriends who always ended up getting beaten senseless in my basement, I came to the sudden realization . . . I'll take him! Much like one would say to a department store employee when discovering an unexpected great deal, "I'll take it." Only in this case it was, "I'll take him!"

It was years before the age that I had vowed my daughter was supposed to be allowed to date, but I kept having nightmares about forbidding my daughter to date this kid that seemed decent and her ending up with some crack smoking, Hip Hop wannabe living in my basement, or even in a meth lab travel trailer. I found myself secretly hoping the neighborhood kid would end up noticing my daughter.

Sometimes I feel like a sell-out, like I'm caving in to the easy way out as a dad. But then I also think, there's nothing wrong with hoping your daughter picks a good man or boy as it were. He still hasn't shown any interest in my daughter other than being friendly and maybe he never will. But I have decided that if a boy seems to have a good head on his shoulders, and can treat my daughter with the respect that is required to date my daughter, I may not be as opposed as I once thought I would be.

42. THE PARENT TEACHER CONFERENCE

Last year, my wife had just arrived at my daughter's school for a parent-teacher conference. This particular parent-teacher conference seemed a bit more important than many of the others we had attended over the years, in that it was with a teacher of a class that my daughter was having trouble in.

On top of the stress created by a meeting with a teacher whose class your daughter was failing, was also the added stress of my wife and I not being certain that this teacher's own teaching skills might be part of the problem as well as my daughter's own negligence. Needless to say, we were not looking forward to what may take place, especially if we felt that the teacher was trying to dodge her own short comings.

As we entered the classroom and sat down in a pair of extremely small student chairs in front of the teacher's desk, we exchanged niceties and began discussing some of the basic facts concerning my daughters failing. The teacher outlined some of the assignments that my daughter had failed to turn in . . . and then, my attention was drawn to a funny tickle coming from inside my left nostril every time I exhaled. It was somewhere in the spectrum between an intense vibration and an itch.

Quickly I pushed the nose tickle to the back of my mind and tried to focus on the very important meeting with the teacher. My wife was responding to the teacher by saying something about my daughter being confused over which of the assignments were due . . . again the tickle in my nose demanded my attention, and I was almost certain that I could hear a faint whistling-flapping sound when I exhaled. It was hard to focus on the discussion taking place between my wife and the teacher. With a little deducing and experimentation with different exhaling velocities, I was able to determine that the source of my irritation was . . . an extraordinarily long nose hair.

As my wife and the teacher traded snarky quips over what a reasonable expectation is for a student getting work done on time, and the proper communication from the teacher concerning clarity on due dates and assignments, I felt the discussion ramp up a notch in tempo. But I still couldn't give the conversation my full attention.

The knowledge that I had a nose hair jutting out from my nostril only made the discomfort worse. Each exhale was becoming increasingly torturous. The offending hair was beat about in the wind like one of those old, wire car antennas that was being subjected to freeway air speeds. The tickle had now become a raging itch that numerous attempts at quelling with a subtle nose rub would not relieve.

The voices of the two women in the background now had the distinct tone of anger in them. The conversation was getting louder.

"AND I THINK YOU NEED TO CLARIFY BETWEEN AN ASSIGNMENT BEING DUE IN THE

MORNING OR SIMPLY BY THE END OF THE DAY!" I heard my wife say in an extremely irritated voice.

The teacher began shooting back an answer in an equally angry tone, while I was trying to figure out a way to relieve my agony. I pinched at my nose several times, trying not to make it obvious what I was trying to do. I nodded my head occasionally to make it seem like I was up to speed with the discussion, but this only made me think I might have caught a glimpse of the long hair waving. I looked down and cross-eyed to confirm whether or not I had actually seen it. I exhaled forcefully. Yep! I could see it. I could make it wave up and down like a trained cobra by exhaling and inhaling in rapid succession, which entertained me momentarily and took my mind off of the intense itch.

Just as my eyes became strained from looking cross-eyed for too long and I felt like I was beginning to hyperventilate, I became aware that neither of the women were talking. In fact, the room was silent. Uncrossing my eyes and looking up, my sight refocused on my wife and the teacher . . . both of them silently staring at me with looks of anger and bewilderment. They seemed less than amused by my cross-eyed downward stare and rapid nostril breathing in the midst of the tense discussion. It probably looked to them like I was simply making ridiculous faces for the fun of it (this is where past history did not work in my favor).

"I . . ." but before I could begin my explanation, the disturbance in my nose shot a huge sneeze out of my face so rapidly and unexpectedly, that my hand had barely begun to travel towards my head in attempt to cover my nose and mouth.

"AAAACHHHOOOOO!!!"

The sneeze had escaped full force without my being able to stifle it or divert its trajectory in any way. The nasal explosion disturbed several papers on the teacher's desk and left the air glistening under the bright fluorescent lights with a fine sneeze mist that encompassed the entire area that the three of us occupied. My wife and the teacher covered their faces and tried to get out from underneath the cloud, but to no avail.

"OH FOR THE LOVE OF . . .," the teacher started to say with disgust.

Using the sneeze as an excuse to bring my hand up to my nose, I frantically searched for the nose hair, pinching at the area beneath my left nostril in hopes of snagging the troublesome nose gremlin. And much to my surprise and joy, I seemed to have gotten ahold of it with one of my blind grabs.

"AHAAAA!" I exclaimed triumphantly, and gave a solid tug.

With the sound of a high pitched guitar string breaking, the hair let loose of its inner nostril real estate, causing me to wince in pain and relief. My eyes instantly began to water profusely, and I could feel a second, more powerful sneeze rocketing towards my face.

"WHAAAACHOOOOOOOO!"

The air was once again glistening with sneeze shrapnel, but at this point I didn't care.

"I got it . . . SEEE?!" I wheezed, wiping my tear streaked cheeks and holding up the inch and a half long hair for my wife and my daughter's teacher to see. "I'm all good now!"

"I think I'm beginning to see where some of the problems originate," the teacher said coldly, and then got up from her chair and left the room.

"YOU MORON!" My wife sneered, and then punched me on the arm harder than I can ever remember being punched. She stood up and left the classroom, following the lead of the teacher.

I guess I can see why the both of them were so annoyed, but they need to understand that I was as much a victim of the situation as they were, if not more!

My wife finished her conference with the teacher later that week without bothering to invite me. In fact, the night of the nose hair attack ended up being the last parent-teacher conference I have attended to this day. In some ways I feel like I had been rail-roaded by karma, but then, I never really liked going to those conferences anyhow.

43. GLORY DAYS

There are a percentage of fathers, such as myself, who feel that it might be best if they do not reveal the entire details of what they would describe as their "wild and crazy days" to their children while they are of a certain young age. Or if they do, it might be best that they not glorify such days in a sentimental light or one that might suggest that it had been fun.

In other words, we try to refrain from reminiscing about high school parties that ended in farm implements being submerged in swimming pools, police, fire department, and secret service being called, an apology to the owner of a local petting zoo being issued by the mayor, and some town residents moving to Detroit because they felt it would be safer.

In the event that we are caught talking about such glory days by our children, we quickly add something like, "Uh, yeah, that really sucked, I'm glad that we've outgrown that nonsense."

It's not like we want to lie to our kids, or even hide truth from them. It just seems that's some war stories that are better suited for telling when they get older and hopefully can see the foolishness of such antics.

Hopefully, by the time we do feel comfortable telling our kids about all of our less than stellar moments of our youth, they will be able to learn from them as well as being amused. And heaven forbid they are able to match our stories with their own, or worse yet, have tales that top our foolishness.

44. FINANCES

I have been writing these silly little stories for several years now. And in all those years, and all those stories, I have yet to write one on finances. The subject has only been mentioned in stories.

While I was pondering my lack of addressing an issue that is so central to the functioning, or lack of functioning, of a family, I realized that I probably hadn't done a story about finances because I like my stories to have a direction. Our finances over the years have gone in several directions. It is much easier to write about the success of our money managing system, almost as an instructional piece. Or it would be easy to write about the disasters of our money mismanagement, more like a tragic comedy, or a cautionary tale. But our finances don't seem to follow either direction for any significant length of time.

We have had periods of what seemed like great prosperity, where we not only paid our bills, but had money left over for things like vacations and shoes and supreme pizzas instead of just pepperoni.

But we have also had lean times, where we weren't sure how the mortgage was going to be paid and groceries were being put on a credit card.

I guess to a financial advisor, these extremes would be clear evidence that our money managing does have a direction and that it's not a particularly good one. Yet we have always managed to pay our bills, and even been able to work down some debt during the times of prosperity. So it wouldn't seem like our direction could be quite considered disastrous.

I know that we need to sit down and figure out a budget that works, but every time we do, there will surely be something that comes along and shatters our budget into a million pieces. And then out of frustration, we fall back into "winging it."

By now some of you are smacking your foreheads and thinking, "You are saying exactly what the problem is! You need a budget that evens out these financial waves and provides savings that will cover disasters in the lean times!"

And don't think I am not aware of this.

I've figured out the basic problem with our budget keeping. The budget is designed to carry over funds that are the extra from times of abundance to times of need. This allows us to pay for the unexpected costs that destroy a budget when times are more "paycheck to paycheck." The problem comes during the periods of having a little extra. The speed at which you can spend it on things that seem so inconsequential is amazing!

Times are good so we ...

Buy caramel lattes at Starbucks instead of making coffee at home ... $18 a week.

Eat out one more time a month that usual because we deserve it ... $42 a month.

Go through car wash instead of using the garden hose ... $10 a week.

Add a movie channel or two to the cable bill . . . $22 a month.

Buy extra songs from iTunes . . . $53 a month.

New Pink Floyd poster to replace the one my wife ripped yanking it down from the living room wall during the great decorating war of 2011 . . . $14.

Take on a car payment because I'm sick of working on the cobbled together junkers that we can afford to buy with cash . . . $355 a month.

Buy new socks, underwear, bras, tires, toasters, lawn mowers, printers, DVD players and brake pads when they are worn out instead of trying to nurse them along for another year . . . $50 to $876 a month.

And yet after all that extra money, you haven't really improved your quality of life, well, except for the Pink Floyd poster. It doesn't really seem like we are spending more. It's not like we are spending extravagantly.

It's probably a good thing that I did sit down and write this frustrating rant on finances. It has motivated me to buckle down and stick to a budget that actually works. I am done spending on all those little extra things that add up.

Well, maybe with the exception of the caramel lattes and maybe the occasional iTunes song and the supreme pizza instead of pepperoni. But that's it! Nothing else!

45. THE ICY ROAD BRAKE TEST

Each winter signals the start to the 'hazardous driving condition' season in Michigan and consequently the employment of a technique I call "testing the roads."

The testing of the roads requires that I (the tester) stomp the brakes sharply several times, while simultaneously turning the steering wheel from side to side. I can then judge the traction of the tires on the road by observing the resulting movement of my wife (the test subject). If her head jerks dramatically forward and back, and violently side to side, it would indicate that the traction is good, thus stopping and turning shouldn't be a problem. However, if the test produces minimum head movement, other than her turning towards me to shoot me a laser like glare of disapproval, accompanied by her emitting a hissing sound with a robust gripping of the center arm rest and door handle, it can be concluded that road conditions may be icy.

My wife is not at all a fan of my testing methods, even in spite of the test's effectiveness being proven time and time again. In fact it has been the cause of many arguments. And I can't say with a clear conscience that I haven't thrown in a few extra brake pedal stomps for the simple amusement of watching her head move involuntarily. But generally, the procedure is strictly an information gathering maneuver.

Normally, our winter vehicle of choice was a full sized, four wheel drive truck. I find that the weight, wheel base and height of the vehicle combined with the fact that it is four wheel drive provides us with the best chances of making it through the winter driving season with the least amount of difficulty. Recently with the increasing price of gasoline, combined with my having to drive quite a bit farther to work due to a transfer, resulted in my purchasing a much smaller, non-four wheel drive vehicle with better gas mileage.

The new smaller vehicle was indeed a relief when it came to my weekly gas expense, but with the unexpected early arrival of winter, it left me in need of a recalibrating to the the icy road test results data interpretation. Without my truck and its' familiarity in winter driving conditions, I felt as if I was driving blind.

One of the first days of icy precipitation, my wife and I happened to be heading over to visit a family member who lived an hour from our home. As we sped down the freeway, what started out as a light rain began to have a bit more of a solid sound as it landed on the windshield. The digital thermometer on the car's dash also indicated that the temperature had fallen to thirty-one degrees. As we travelled on, the grass on the sides of the freeway began to become covered with an icy snow and up ahead, it looked like the first ditch victim of the season had slid into the freeway's median.

"I think it might be getting icy" my wife exclaimed in an audibly nervous voice.

"Oh, I doubt it. People just forget how to drive each year. It's just the idiots that end up in the ditch on days like this. It's hardly snowing."

But to make sure, I decided to assess the conditions with a testing of the roads.

As was normal for a testing, I gave three quick powerful stomps to the brake, and turned the steering wheel from right to left. Instinctively, I watched my wife's head, expecting to see it dip sharply towards the dashboard followed by it moving from side to side in a motion like she was swaying to one of her favorite songs.

Much to my surprise, her head made no motion at all. In fact, she wouldn't have even been aware of my testing of the roads had she not heard my foot hit the brake pedal and watched as I cranked from side to side on the steering wheel.

We were driving seventy miles an hour on what would be the equivalent to an ice skating pond.

"YOU IDIOT!" my wife yelled, piercing my face with the familiar daggers of angry disapproval.

But I had more pressing matters to contend with than her deadly glare. The icy roads, combined with my test procedure in an unfamiliar vehicle resulted in our ever so gradual spinning to the right. My standing on the brake did not slow or correct the slow motion slide at all, in fact, it almost felt like we sped up a little.

Within the few seconds of time it took for me to turn to my wife and ask if we still had towing service included in our insurance policy, the car had rotated ninety degrees from its normally facing forward position. We were now travelling at seventy miles an hour down the freeway . . . sideways. Scenery was now moving from the left side of the windshield to the right in a blur, instead of the normal coming straight at us.

Just as I was marveling at the strange sensation caused by travelling down the freeway sideways at a high rate of speed, I heard the familiar hiss of my wife going into panic mode followed by the *Whump, Whump* of her hands assuming their death grip on the door handle and the center arm rest.

Instantly, I was aware of an intense pain shooting throughout my entire body. For a split second, the pain caused me some confusion as to what was causing it. But a quick bit of investigation and the use of rudimentary geometry skills resulted in my concluding that when my wife's left hand had come down with a *Whump* to assume its panicked, white knuckle grasp of the center arm rest, it hadn't landed on the center arm rest at all. There was no center arm rest in the smaller new car! Due to her now sitting a foot or two closer to me than she had in the larger trucks of the past, her hand had landed squarely in the middle of my lap, where it instinctively held on for dear life. She held on for dear life to the one part of the male anatomy that a male would least likely want to have held on to for dear life.

"UUGHHYYEEEEOOOOWWW!" I managed to groan in pain, slumping forward.

"JON! JON! JON!" my wife shouted, locked in a record-skipping frame of mind caused by shear panic and terror.

"LET GO! LET GO! LET GO!" I answered, but her grip only increased as the lazy rotation of the car now had us travelling backwards down the freeway at seventy miles an hour.

Letting go of the steering wheel, I grabbed her arm and tried to pry her hand from that which made me a man.

With great difficulty, I was finally able to free myself from her vice like claws. For the second it took for her to reclaim a grip, this time on my shirt, it also included a handful of chest hair. The pain of the hair being pulled was still intense, but compared to the crushing of my man parts, it had lessened in severity enough for me to return my hands to the steering wheel.

Due to the fact that the car was now sliding backwards, we were now face to face with the people in the car behind us, which was still travelling in a frontward direction. I could see the driver's mouth hanging open in astonishment at our predicament. The passenger was a teenage girl who was holding up her cell phone, apparently videoing our unfortunate circumstances.

"Huh, I wonder if we'll make it on to the World's Craziest Drivers show," I pondered aloud to my wife who was now catatonic from terror.

Just then, the smooth sound of the tires sliding across the icy pavement was replaced with a much harsher, gravelly sound, indicating that the car was now leaving the pavement, and sliding into the median. Through my backward view out the windshield, I could see dirt, grass and snow flying up in the air. I shut my eyes tightly and clenched the steering wheel in anticipation of hitting something behind us, or in front of us as it were.

And then, everything went silent, there was no longer the sensation that we were moving. I looked over at my wife who was white with fear and clutching a small piece of t-shirt material and a handful of hair. I looked down at the fist-sized hole in my shirt that framed what looked like a freshly waxed chest.

Making sure my wife was not hurt, I quickly exited the car and ran to the rear, where the lingering pain from my groin and chest caused me to vomit.

As I tried to check for injuries without actually pulling my pants down in front of the freeway traffic audience, I noticed that sheerly by chance, we had crash landed only a hundred feet beyond the car in the ditch that I had spotted up ahead of us just prior to going into our own slide. The driver had already begun making his way towards me to see if we were ok.

In the hour it took for the tow truck to arrive and pull both cars out of the median, I learned that the name of the other car's driver was Henry, and that he too had been performing a testing of the road conditions that went awry.

My wife spent most of the hour in the very nice Cadillac belonging to Henry, where she and Henry's wife traded angry condemnations of our road testing methods. They had the doors locked and refused to let my new friend Henry and myself inside the plush vehicle.

Henry and I sat in my more modest gas saving car listening to Spanish music on the radio with a broken tuning knob and asking each other things like, "How mad do you think they really are? I mean, we were only trying to see if the roads were icy!"

At long last the tow truck arrived and was able to get both cars back onto the shoulder of the road.

After hugs and goodbyes to Henry and his wife, we set out once again. Only this time my wife was driving. I had been banished to the back seat to think about my road testing and to try to replace the material that my wife had removed from my shirt with some safety pins.

46. BECAUSE I LOVE HER

I will change my T-shirt socks and underwear daily, even though I'm sure they would last another day or maybe two before becoming too offensive.

I will get up from my spot on the couch and get her a cup of coffee when she asks me to, even though she is actually closer and already standing . . . but I might complain a little.

I will put the toilet seat down.

I will resist the temptation to explode in a violently child-like tantrum when I come home to find that my drawers, tools and other personal storage places have been "organized." This of course means that some of my items will have disappeared into the great void of space forever.

I will spend an entire weekend standing on a five gallon bucket being sprayed by the fine mist of teal paint slinging off of the paint roller that I am using to apply our living room's new trendy look. Knowing that in less than a year, I will be standing on the same five gallon bucket changing the color of our dining room, or bedroom, or bathroom, only to eventually be followed by painting over the teal in the living room with the latest trendy new color.

47. SATURDAY NIGHT

It's Saturday night. A night that promises a reward for all of the preceding weeks labor. A night for the young-at-heart to cut loose and bend a few rules. It's a night I used to look forward too.

What am I doing this Saturday night? I'm wandering around the Meijer lawn and garden section looking for a lawn mower that I can't afford. I'm drinking coffee at Starbucks and using their WIFI to check my Facebook and email. I'm napping in the front seat of my car with the radio playing.

And what has inspired me to spend my Saturday evening doing such excitement filled activities? I'm killing time while my daughter watches a movie with her friends because it's not worth it to drive all the way home for a half hour and then come back to get her when the movie is over.

That's what my Saturday nights have degraded to. I am no longer one who participates in the joyous activities of a weekend earned. I have become the support staff to my daughter's fun-filled social life.

Yep, I'm rockin' the dad thing.

48. A HORRIFIC TALE ABOUT WRITER'S BLOCK

The urge to write something epic was over-powering. I needed to create a piece that was unique, but still containing all the time tested components of a classic. I could feel the creative genius building inside me like a pile of leaves that had been ignited with too much gasoline.

A novel! I'd write a novel that would put Melville's silly fish story to shame. . . . . No, that would take too long and I know from experience, that these bursts of creative energy only last a few hours, or until something catches my eye on TV.

Maybe a poem . . . no, that's an even more ridiculous notion. I haven't the slightest idea how to meter, and I think I might be rhyme deaf.

So, I decided that I should stop wasting time deciding what form of literature my writing would be, and just start writing. I could always decide later if it was a novel, or poem, or short story. I would just let the spirit take me wherever it wanted.

I sat down at the computer with my cup of coffee. I made myself comfortable, and prepared to unleash the epic-ness . . . I cracked my knuckles in preparation for the flurry of typing . . . here we go.

But nothing was coming out.

The keyboard keys were not clacking.

I thought for sure that this much inspiration was surely the precursor to an earth-shaking subject matter. It hadn't even crossed my mind that I really had no ideas on deck. The desire to begin my masterpiece was unbearable, but there was nothing there!

I began to look around the room as if the dirty cereal bowl on the end table, or the floral print box of Kleenexes would suddenly jar a topic loose but again, there was nothing.

I stood up and scratched my head. I looked out the window at the overgrown lawn, but all that came to mind was that the lawn mower blades needed sharpening. For a second, I pondered a novel about dull lawn mower blades, but it seemed to lack the potential for being the awesomeness that I was determined to create.

Picking up a women's magazine from the coffee table, I began to leaf through it. I would write a story about . . . dish soap? No, that's silly . . . how about "Sizzling Summer Fashion Ideas?" No, even the word fashion itself, made me yawn . . . tampons? Good Lord, NO!

I simply had nothing to write about and it was beginning to make me angry. I was getting angry at my brain. Stupid brain!

After another two hours of seeking ideas from magazines, two glasses of wine, watching the dog sleep, and both sides of Pink Floyd's "Wish You Were Here" album, I finally gave in to the fact that I had no idea what to write about, and all the ambition in the world was simply not going to change that fact.

In an act of desperation, I sat down and began writing about having writer's block, the result of which you are reading now. It certainly isn't the Pulitzer Prize winner that I was anticipating, but it did occupy me until a documentary about South African Crocodiles came on the television.

Unfortunately, I don't think I can get away with writing about having writer's block more than once with any degree of success. I guess the next time I have writer's block you will be stuck reading about a floral print box of Kleenexes.

49. A FEW HELPFUL PARENTING TIPS

*Whenever you find yourself at a loss of words while yelling at your kids, simply start making statements like you are quoting one of the Ten Commandments.
"Thou shalt not give an attitude towards thine parents' wisdom, or hell shalt surely follow."
It catches them off guard if nothing else.

*If you are having trouble getting your kids to clean up their rooms and keep them clean, try getting a box of ten penny nails and nail all objects to the floor where they lay.

*When dealing with a picky eater, try fishing a cat poop out of the litter box and put it on a plate as an alternate choice to what is being served. Often times a shift in perspective can cause the picky eaters to expand their palates. Other alternate dinner choices can include sink strainer gumbo, dog food (be careful though, some kids actually prefer dog food to some dishes), and toe nail trail mix.

*In order to discourage my girls from rolling their eyes after every other sentence that comes out of my mouth, I have taped pictures to the ceiling all over our house. There are pictures of me in skinny jeans, a muscle shirt, flashing pretend gang signs and my hair styled in that Justin Bieber swept forward look. That way, when they do roll their eyes at me, I get the last laugh.

50. LET ME TAKE A SELFIE

I began to notice that my youngest daughter, Natalie, seemed to have a different profile picture on her Facebook page nearly every single day. Most of them were very similar to each other. She would have different clothes on for each shot and there was some variety in the faces she was making, but other than that, they all looked pretty much the same to me.

"Why do you keep posting a new picture of your face every day?" I finally asked her.

"Those are selfies, dad, and that's what you're supposed to do," she answered matter-of-factly.

"Selfie? Supposed to? Why don't you just pick a nice one and leave it, like my profile picture of me holding up the huge Bass I caught?" I wondered.

"Because I don't want to be a nerd who has had the same profile picture for three years like you," she replied in a sarcastic tone, "and Robert told us you didn't even catch that fish. You found it floating dead by the shore and fished it out with a stick."

"Well it seems a little silly and very self-interested to take that many pictures of yourself if you ask me," I said.

At first I simply scoffed at her accusations, but being called nerd kept eating at me. I have never been one to follow the latest trends, but I didn't really like the label. Also, I didn't realize that my neighbor Robert had betrayed me by leaking the truth about the twenty inch Bass that I was proudly holding up in my Facebook profile picture.

After a solid afternoon of pondering the whole "selfie" profile picture issue and my daughter's hurtful words ringing in my ears, I decided it might be time for a change.

Later that evening, my wife took both of our girls out for a shopping trip to the mall. This left me with the perfect opportunity to work on my new picture. So taking cue from the many hundreds of pictures my daughter had taken of herself, I went into the bathroom and stood in front of the mirror.

At first I felt a little silly, even a little vain. But after deciding on a face that I thought looked pleasant with a bit of manly edginess, I took my first selfie.

Upon reviewing my results, I decided on trying another one with a touch more manly edginess and a sprinkle of compassionate rage. The second photo was even better than the first.

I began to experiment a little. I took a selfie sucking in my belly and puffing out my chest . . . ohhh that was a good one. I took one with a mean face. I took two with different wise and respectful expressions. I took one that showed off the scar on my arm that I had sustained while trying to teach the cat and dog to pet each other (which I sometimes told people was a knife scar from my days in a street gang). I even tried one with puffed out lips and sultry eyes like the ones I had seen my daughter take . . . but then quickly deleted it. Before I knew it, and hour had passed and I now had around thirty-five selfies to choose from for my profile picture.

I decided that out of the thirty-five pictures, there should be at least a few that would be worthy of representing me on social media, so I sat down on the couch to pick on one.

After another hour of trying different photo effects and self-debate, I finally decided on my next profile picture and uploaded it. I felt like I had been released from the title of nerd the very second I hit the "done" button, replacing my three year old Bass holding photo.

About two hours later, my wife and daughters returned home from the mall. My youngest daughter burst in the door and dropped her shopping bags on the floor.

"DDDAAAAAADDDD!!!!"

"What?" I answered wondering what I had done wrong.

"Dads aren't supposed to take selfies!!!" she demanded.

Apparently she had already noticed my new profile picture.

"Why not? You are the one who called me a nerd!"

"Because number one, you are a guy. Number two, you are old. And number three, if you are going to take one, you need to make sure the toilet isn't in the background, and if it is for some reason, you really, really need to make sure that it has been flushed. You are so embarrassing. I unfriended you," she yelled and stomped off to her bedroom . . . probably to take a "Dad is so embarrassing" selfie.

Quickly I went through my collection of pictures to find a different shot for my profile. Of the thirty-five pictures I had taken of myself, all of them but two had the toilet in the background, and those two were close ups with what I called my "happy lunatic" face. So I settled on one with a rather plain facial expression that had the toilet (but was at an angle that kept the viewer from seeing its contents) and replaced the offending profile picture.

Throughout the next few days, when I found myself alone, I decided to reshoot some of the better selfies, making sure that the toilet was nowhere to be seen.

On my way to town, I took a few more while driving. I took some at work and while mowing the lawn. I had to admit, I was getting pretty good at it.

Near the end of the week, as I was setting up for my "I'm the lead singer to Led Zeppelin" selfie shoot, I was suddenly confronted with a message on my phone screen that said, "Memory card is full."

"POOP!" I exclaimed to myself. I had just spent twenty minutes getting the lighting and background just perfect for my selfie session, and now my phone was full. I became distressed at the thought of wasting all that prep time, just to be shut down by a bloated memory card. So I decided to delete some of my lesser favorite pictures to make room.

But as I went through my gallery, I was having trouble deciding which selfies to sacrifice. Even the ones I didn't like as much as others seemed to have elements that made them irreplaceable.

There was the selfie on my mower where I had my eyes closed, but also had a squirrel in the background that looked like he was giving a peace sign. There was selfie taken while unintentionally running a red light, followed by selfie pulled over on the side of the road with cop car behind me. I thought about giving up a series of selfies I took while sitting on the toilet, but I liked the way the downward angle made it look like my hairline hadn't receded as far as it had. And there was no way I was getting rid of my selfies taken while arguing with my wife, I liked the honesty of my angry expressions in that set. I decided that instead of deleting any of my cherished collection, I would make a flying trip to the store for a bigger memory card.

When I arrived back home excited to begin my Led Zeppelin selfie session, I was met inside the front door by my wife who was holding the microphone I had constructed out of a broom handle with a flashlight duct taped to the end.

"You are out of control!" she huffed.

"You are just still mad about the selfies I took while we were arguing!" I shot back.

In an act of pure spite, she ripped the flashlight microphone off the end of the broomstick microphone stand and threw them on the floor. Instantly we began arguing.

The loud commotion soon got the attention of my daughters, who joined in the fight on the side of my wife.

After an hour of rather intense yelling and an attempt to get at least one good selfie in the midst of the fray, I was finally beaten down. It was decided by the members of the family who were not me that I would only be allowed one selfie per day. And it was also decided that any new profile pictures that I wanted to post, had to be approved by a member of the family that was also not me.

Once the arguing had subsided and I had admitted defeat, I begrudgingly deconstructed my Led Zeppelin stage and then locked myself in the bathroom. I then spent my one daily selfie on one I call my "You guys don't understand me and have no idea how hard the life of a middle-aged dad is" selfie.

51. DADS, DAUGHTERS, AND BOYFRIENDS

As a rule, dads don't generally like boyfriends. We love to make threats about what will happen to them if they hurt our daughters, or step out of bounds. These threats often involve shotguns and unmarked graves located in the swamp. We are unmercifully critical of them, and we are unlikely to cut them any slack whatsoever.

This is probably not much different than how parents of boys feel about their potential girlfriends. And I'm sure there will be parents who are as skeptical of my girls as I am about their boys. But being the father of two girls, I can only write about how I view boyfriends.

One reason for this universal hatred of boyfriends is the thought of these little hormone gremlins doing unimaginable things to our daughters that shouldn't happen until she is married, which shouldn't be a day before her thirty-fifth birthday. Unfortunately, every dad was once a hormone gremlin himself. We know how they think. We know how they operate.

And it cannot be overlooked that teenage girls can be encouragers of the hormone gremlins. Teenage girls are quick to learn the power they hold over boys. This makes for a deadly combination, and it is for this reason that we are ever vigilant and suspicious of their every action.

Another reason for us to persecute boyfriends is perhaps to weed out the weaker ones from the pack. In my mind, there is no boy worthy of my daughter's hand in marriage. But knowing that her getting married is inevitable, I do my best to make sure our daughter ends up with the best husband possible.

But when I really sit and think about it, there is yet another reason beyond the other obvious ones, that dads hate boyfriends so much. That reason is simply not being willing to give up the monopoly that a dad holds on being their daughter's hero. A boyfriend is someone who might eventually end up stealing that title.

I mean who is this punk that he thinks he can just come in here and win my daughters heart with nothing more than his cocky sense of humor and his seventy-five dollar pair of baggy jeans?

Where was he when she was a baby? It wasn't him who cleaned up all those poopy diapers or walked her for countless midnight hours while she screamed at the top of her lungs. Where was he for all those skinned knees, bruises, and hurt feelings that I comforted her through? Where was he when her first hamster died and together we held a backyard funeral service? He wasn't the one who had protected her and kept her from harm for the last sixteen years. He hadn't even come close to earning an equal place in my daughter's heart. It's not fair for him to even have a chance!

Then I remember that I was once that punk kid showing up at another father's doorstep . . . hoping to steal the affections of his daughter. I have to stop and tell myself that whichever one of these annoying punks' ends up winning my daughter as his wife may not have earned the right to be her hero as much as I had, but maybe only because he hadn't had the chance yet.

So as painful as it may be, I realize that I must grant this Johnny-come-lately temporary permission to be my baby girl's hero. I will give him a chance to earn the title. I will allow him the opportunity to become my daughter's protector and comforter. And later still, to become everything I was to my daughter, with his own son or daughter . . . my grandchild.

So whichever one of you my daughter ends up picking, take this temporary permission that I give, and use it wisely. Earn the right to be called my daughter's hero, and the hero of my grandchildren. Because if you squander this chance, or fail to live up to this title, you will have me to deal with, and the stories involving shotguns and shallow graves in a swamp, may end up not being just stories after all.

52. OVERDOSE

I can't figure out if my wife is trying to kill me, or if my near death incidents due to drug overdoses are simply accidents. I don't have a large life insurance policy, so I can't figure out why she would want me dead, but there have been incidents that would make a person wonder.

One such incident occurred when I had developed an extremely agonizing kidney stone. After a flying trip to the hospital, I was given a powerful pain medication and sent on my way. My wife, who is a nurse, took charge of my pill bottle. Upon arriving home, she handed me my first dose to take before the morphine that I had been given at the hospital had a chance to wear off.

Since there was nothing for me to do other than take the pain medication and wait for the kidney stone to run its course, we decided not to cancel the dinner plans we had made with another couple earlier that week.

By the time we had arrived at the restaurant where our dinner engagement was to take place, the pain medication had begun to take effect. I not only was pain-free, but I felt good. I felt REALLY good. We greeted our friends in the parking lot and went inside.

The hostess who looked remarkably like a female version of the Joker from Batman, showed us to our table where a waiter who looked remarkably like the Penguin brought us menus and drinks.

It was at this time that I suddenly realized what a funny guy I was. I made myself laugh just thinking about it. Everyone else was remarkably funny as well, so I laughed even harder. My wife gave me a frown, a very funny frown.

I could hear the voice of our friend, only it sounded like his head was in a steel barrel submerged somewhere in the sea.

"Is he alright?" the voice said.

"He's fine," said the walrus that was now seated between me and my wife.

Removing my shirt, I wrapped it tightly around my head and ears to block out the ringing and the obnoxious sound of the Christmas carol singing unicorns. The last thing I remember was biting the waiter's leg from under the table.

As I slowly opened my eyes, they focused on one of our friends leaning over me and fanning my face with her small handbag. I could tell that I was in the passenger seat of our car in the parking lot of the restaurant.

"His eyes are opening!"

I turned to see my wife looking intently at my bottle of pain pills and talking to the husband of the woman fanning my face.

"He's lucky to be alive! He's only supposed to be taking two pills every four hours," I heard my friend say emphatically to my wife.

"I thought it said four pills every two hours!" answered my wife's voice.

As I recalled later that day, I remembered thinking it was odd that a prescription required me to take four pills all at once. I don't ever remember taking more than two of any medication at a time.

My wife had nearly killed me.

Now if this had been the only time that medication handed out by my wife had almost killed me, it would be easier to assume that it was a simple mistake. But a very similar incident occurred just a few months later.

My wife and I had always dreamed of taking an Alaskan cruise and this was the year that we were finally able to afford to do it. So along with a few other friends of ours, we booked our trip. To begin the cruise meant taking a flight from Detroit to Seattle. This presented a problem, as I do not like flying at all.

As the day of our flight grew closer, I became more and more panicked. My wife decided to talk to my doctor about my phobia, and he prescribed a rather powerful anti-anxiety medication to make the trip less stressful for both me and my wife who would be sitting next to me.

On the morning we were due to fly out to Seattle, we arrived at the airport and found our places in the luggage check-in line. My nervousness was beginning to make me sweat and act in a fashion that was described by my wife as "flakey." While we stood waiting, my wife handed me one of the pills which I quickly swallowed.

The pill had definitely calmed my anxiety. I experienced the entire flight in slow motion, or at least the parts of the flight that I was not unconscious. The drug seemed like a bit of over kill, but they did get me to Seattle without a complete nervous breakdown.

After an amazing week-long vacation that went by entirely too fast, we found ourselves once again waiting in an amazingly long line at the airport. And once again, I began to feel nervous and flakey.

"Do you want a whole one?" my wife asked me referring to the medication.

"Yes!" I replied hoping it would take the edge off.

I quickly took the pill and continued our hour long wait in the security screening line.

I was surprised at how much faster the tranquilizer took effect compared to the morning of our flight out to Seattle. I soon found it difficult to stand in line without swaying.

"Wow, I must be tired. It seems like the pill is hitting me a little harder than last time," I said to my wife in a voice that sounded like a record being played at too slow of a speed.

"Well yeah, you only took a half of one last time."

I suddenly became aware of my wife using the word "whole" when she asked me if I wanted a "whole" pill . . . as opposed to the half pill I took a week ago. The half pill had bordered on too much. Now I had taken a whole pill and I still had to stand in line for at least an hour before we could board the plane.

I turned towards my wife with heavy eyes and informed her that I may be in trouble. The now familiar sound of Christmas carols began to fill the air as the unicorns floated down from the ceiling and formed a circle around me. I tried sitting on one our larger suitcases when the line wasn't moving, but I kept fading out, only to return when the large man behind me would smack me in the head for leaning and drooling on him. The unicorns were joined by Richard Nixon who was wearing a beautiful sun dress and together they kept me entertained with their festive music.

By the time we neared the security check point, one of our friends who had accompanied us on the cruise had found an airport wheelchair to push me in as we moved up the line because it was easier than dragging me. I sat and happily sang *Silent Night* with the unicorns and faded in and out of consciousness.

Finally reaching the security screening check point, the man checking passengers' identification looked down at me and asked, "Is he ok? Do I need to call the medics?"

"Oh I'm wonderful," I heard myself say, "I'm on drugs and my wife is trying to kill me."

Fortunately, I faded away at this point, and slept blissfully through the additional two hours of questioning that my statement had caused us.

Now I suppose I could just assume that another dosage miscalculation had taken place, but two, in the same year? Until I can determine whether my wife is out to get me or not, I am assuming full and complete control of all my medication.

If she doesn't actually want me dead, she must certainly be gaining some sort of amusement by sending me to sing with the unicorns.

53. WHEN I WAS GROWING UP

When I was growing up, we didn't have iPods and Pandora. If you wanted songs from your favorite band, you sat a tape recorder in front of the stereo speaker, and waited until one of "your" songs came on, and then hit the record button. Then you had to try and stop the recording before the annoying DJ talked all over the end of your song.

When I was growing up, if I had a report due, it meant spending a day at the library. You poured over books with paper pages and had to operate a multi-drawer collection of about eighty thousand small note cards called an index file that someone named Dewey invented. Or if you were lucky, your family had a set of 1947 encyclopedias that could provide just enough information to squeak through a report, in spite of the large bulk of the information being outdated and the volumes smelling like a musty basement. We weren't able to sit on our bed with a laptop using the internet to deliver every imaginable fact available, while we munched on Doritos and listened to Eminem.

When I was growing up, we had Lawn Jarts that could put holes into the skulls of kids and sun heated steel slides that delivered third degree burns to a child before being emptied onto pavement that removed layers of skin instantly. And, no one had ever heard of a bicycle helmet.

When I was growing up, a text was something you wrote on a scrap of paper with a pencil and threw or passed it to the recipient in class. We had face time instead of Facebook, meaning, if you wanted to check on someone's status, you had to walk up to them and ask them. And there was no such thing as a "selfie." Camera film and developing cost way too much to be wasting photo's on things like that. Photos were generally planned and commemorated an event.

When I was growing up, we got bullied the old fashioned way, with a punch to the head and a kick to the crotch. There was no such thing as cyber bullying.

I say all these things like I am disgusted with the way things are today. But I have to imagine my father was saying similar things about my generation having color TV, Atari, and Sony Walk-mans. So I apologize if I sound like I'm complaining. I'm merely taking on the role that every father since the dawning of time has taken on. And likewise, our sons and daughters will complain about the things that have changed from when they were kids and things were so much tougher.

54. THE POWER OUTAGE

The living room lights and television flickered and then went dark. The ice storm that had started in the early morning hours had finally claimed our electricity.

I had been forewarned by nearly a week of weather updates, and I had considered buying a generator. But it always seems like these impending weather disasters never seem to end up as the apocalyptic disasters that they are advertised to be by the weather man, and generators are expensive. Apparently, they called this storm correctly.

My yard was now a disaster zone of ice laden tree limbs and even entire trees. But that was a problem for later days. The most pressing problem was our lack of electricity, which also meant no heat or water.

"We'll just camp out in the living room," my wife said cheerfully.

I wasn't nearly as excited as my wife about the prospect of camping out, but a call to the power company left me with no expectations of getting our power back in any less than three or four days. There were not many options left to us other than to camp out.

"I guess we're camping out," I groaned in response.

I located my camp cook stove in the shed and brought it into the living room. I ignited the burner and cracked a window to prevent us from all waking up dead. Then, I hung blankets between the living room and kitchen as well as over the hallway entrance to hold in the little heat that it produced.

My wife returned from a trip to the house of a friend who still had power. She had taken every container and bucket we owned to fill with water for toilet flushing and other water necessities.

The water containers were stacked in the dining room and candles were lit to dimly illuminate our camping space. My daughter Hannah had gathered a stack of board games and books to keep us all entertained, and my wife had brought home a monster pile of hot dogs and marshmallows to cook over the camp stove, which seemed to be keeping our living room-tent at a balmy fifty-eight. So bundled with sweatshirts, knit hats and blankets, we settled in for the duration.

The first order of business was to establish the rules of our imprisonment. No opening the refrigerator to prevent the cold from escaping. Make sure the blanket barriers that block off the kitchen and hallway were not breached in order to keep the heat from escaping. And finally, due to limited flush water, it was decreed that when it came to toilet usage, the rule was, "if it's yellow, let it mellow, if it's brown, send it down." (A rule the girls joyfully turned into a song.)

Much to my pleasant surprise, the remainder of the evening was actually kind of fun. We played games and roasted our hotdogs and marshmallows. We laughed and all got along better than when we had power.

When it was time to sleep, we all lined up on a giant makeshift bed on the floor that was made from every blanket and pillow that could be found in the house. We all fell asleep quite quickly.

The first thing I noticed when I awoke was that our living room-tent was freezing cold, and I didn't hear the sound of the camp stove burning. Apparently it had run out of propane.

The second thing I noticed is that my wife and daughters must have decided, at some point during the night, that I was the next best heat source after the camp stove had gone out. All three bodies were plastered against me like stickers on a car bumper. There was a foot on my face, several unidentified appendages lying across the length of my body, and both of my arms and left leg were pinned under the dead weight of wife or daughter carcasses.

After an intense struggle to free myself, I was able to replace the empty propane canister and ignite the camp stove. The rest of the family began to slowly rise, as I prepared our breakfast of cereal, hot dogs and marshmallows.

When we had finished breakfast, the game playing and book reading continued, but with a little bit less laughing and joking than what had been the case the night before. It still wasn't all that bad, just not quite as fun.

By that afternoon, the games were over. We had played every board game we had in the house at least once. And the spirit of good sportsmanship had been replaced by the spirit of sore losers and cheaters. The indigestion of our hot dog and marshmallow lunch was not helping improve the attitudes of our happy campers either. Moral seemed to be taking a turn for the worse. Crabbiness was slowly creeping into the living room-tent.

That evening, as we began to roast our hot dog and marshmallow dinner, a fight over whose turn it was to use the fluffy blue comforter quickly blossomed into and all out shouting match between the four of us. Even the dog barked his grievances.

After an hour of futile shouting and screaming that left none of the complainants feeling like they had accomplished anything, we found ourselves sitting silently in the flickering candle light. The mere clearing of one's throat or heavy breathing would draw the immediate criticism from the other three. I decided that something must be done. The Lord of the Flies had taken over our camp, and I feared the situation was becoming dangerous.

The next day, after our breakfast of hot dogs and marshmallows, I announced that I was venturing out in search of a generator. I knew from phone calls that I had made from the first day of the power outage, that there would be none located anywhere near our county, but I was prepared to travel as far as it took to obtain one. So after a long lecture on being extra considerate to the other members of the camp, I left.

After six hours of searching and making phone calls, I was able to locate a small generator at a hardware store seventy two miles away. Without even thinking about it twice, I purchased the machine and headed back home hoping that all campers there had survived the day without the morality of the troops degrading into violent acts.

Upon arriving home, I cautiously entered the front door where I was greeted by a steady stream of highly irritated sounding female voices. I was grateful that they were still alive and that my generator search had spared me from being in the midst of the fray for the better part of the day.

"I found a generator!" I announced proudly.

The three combatants stopped yelling and looked at me silently for a moment. Then as if I had said nothing, they continued their arguing as if I was not even there. I decided it was best to just get the generator set up and running. It appeared that none of them had weapons, so I figured I had a little time before the disagreements turned deadly.

The generator I had purchased was quite small. I calculated that it had enough power to run two large items such as an electric heater, the water pump, the refrigerator, and electric skillet. Or I could choose one large item and several smaller items, such as lights and electronics.

After careful consideration, I determined that the best configuration to ensure that all campers survived each other was to power the electric heater, a few lights . . . and the television.

Once the generator had purred to life, I ran an extension cord through the window and past the arguing females. Without even being noticed, I plugged in the small heater which began producing a wonderful glow of heat. Then I plugged in a few of the lamps in the living room and turned them on. This seemed to get the attention of the others for a moment, before they went right back to shouting.

Finally, I plugged in the TV and cable box. Instantly the room fell silent. Finding the remote, I switched the channel to one of the few shows that our entire family actually agrees on, and sat down.

No one said an unkind word for the rest of the evening, or any words for that matter. We all sat silent, basking in the blue, hypnotic glow of cable TV. We were civilized again.

I suppose I should feel bad that our family requires a TV to be able to live together in peace, and to be honest, it does bother me a bit. But I take some comfort in the fact that we did do fairly well for the first twenty-four hours. I think we might have made it even longer, had we been able to eat something other than hot dogs and marshmallows for five straight meals. Also, the inability of my camp stove to warm up the living room completely only added to everyone's edginess.

But I do credit the TV for preventing unnecessary violent acts from being committed for the remainder of our time without power. And from now on, it will be one of the first things to be powered by the generator when we lose electricity.

55. DAD FASHION

I have always tended to lean towards practicality when it comes to clothing choices. For instance, I like plain black pocket T-shirts. They are not only cheap, but plain black never goes out of style, or comes in to style either. And with T-shirts, one can always rip off a sleeve or the pocket if you find yourself in a toilet paperless situation. You wouldn't catch someone wearing an eighty dollar "Affliction" T-shirt ripping off the sleeve to use as toilet paper.

Nicer button up shirts are an annoying but necessary evil for times when a T-shirt just isn't dressy enough. I tend to pick button up shirts in colors that best match the color of pet hair that will end up covering it. I also like to keep specialty colors on hand as well. If we are going out to a nice Italian restaurant, I will wear my marinara red shirt.

One of my favorite fashion accessories is the baseball hat. I have several to choose from. I use them in conjunction with my many zippered hoody sweatshirts to accent the looks of different outfits, much like a woman picking out which handbag goes the best with the dress she is wearing. I have hats and hoodies for cold weather, warm weather, work, play, and formal.

I have never owned a suit. I have a matching black shirt, dress pants and tie that I use for weddings and funerals. I bought a pair of vinyl dress shoes twenty years ago that still look like new thanks to several touch ups with a can of black spray paint. You could hardly tell them apart from a two hundred dollar pair of shoes. I just have to remember to perform the touch ups a week before I need to wear them to prevent making myself and those around me from becoming high from the fumes (what a funeral that turned out to be).

56. A CASE OF MISTAKEN IDENTITY

As I finished the last of my five taco lunch that has become a tradition every Wednesday at a little Mexican restaurant near us, I felt the familiar rumble of digestive discontent. I knew from experience, that the ecstasy of my weekly taco fiesta also came with a fair amount of indigestion for the several hours that followed. Quickly I paid my bill, and headed out to my car for a dose of the antacid that I kept for just such situations.

Upon opening the glove box and grabbing the bottle of liquid taco relief, I was dismayed to find the bottle was completely empty. This was a problem. There was serious trouble brewing. I feared there may be an accident if the Mexican fire, which had been ignited by the tacos, was not extinguished soon.

I started the car and headed towards the nearest drug store to purchase a new bottle of antacid. My stomach began to cramp and make strange noises, as if to let me know that time was running out, and beads of sweat had begun to gather on my forehead as I pulled into the drug store parking lot.

Walking briskly, I entered the store and headed straight for the aisle where the antacids were. By now, the gas pain coursing through my abdomen was excruciating. I located a bottle of my preferred stomach relief and headed just as briskly back towards the cash register. When I reached the cash register, I was happy to find only one lady in front of me in the checkout line.

"And of course my son is better than all of the other players on the team, so I just can't understand why he sits on the bench for so much of the game..." said the lady ahead of me in line.

It was obvious that she had already completed her transaction and was now just standing in my way chatting with the drug store employee. For another two minutes, she prattled on, telling the counter lady about her dog being sprayed a skunk, the mailman not closing the door to her mailbox, and a new recipe that she was planning on trying for dinner. The pain in my stomach made her inconsideration even less tolerable than normal.

"Come on lady! I got a situation here!" I finally blurted out of desperation.

With an extremely icy glare, the motor-mouthed lady snapped, "Well, excuse me Mr. Rude Pants!" She then stepped to the side a little so that I could pay for my bottle of taco elixir. I quickly completed my transaction and ran to the door of the building, opening and chugging from the bottle the moment I stepped outside. Finally, the pain began to ease a bit and the gurgling slowed to a whisper, so I continued to my car and got in.

Once inside, my stomach let out a loud growl, and I felt the immense pressure of a large volume of gas move down the intestinal tract. Ever so cautiously, I leaned to one side in the car seat, and let loose the largest volume of the most violently rank smelling gas that my body had ever produced. The fumes were nauseating.

To keep from passing out, I reached down to turn the key on so that I could roll down the windows. But much to my surprise, the keys were not in the ignition.

"Where the heck are my keys?" I wondered aloud. I almost never took my keys out of the ignition, and I certainly wouldn't have thought to do so in the midst of a taco crisis situation. Then, looking over at the passenger seat, I was even more surprised to see a purse sitting there. I noticed that someone had apparently cleaned and vacuumed the inside of my car as well. There were no French fries on the floor mats.

I sat in silent confusion for a minute. Inside my head, the brain cells used to figure out mysteries and math problems slowly decided to wake up and look around. They began to piece together the facts and formulate an answer to what was going on. When the brain cells had completed the necessary calculations, the answer came scrolling across the display screen inside my mind. It read, "You are sitting in the wrong car!"

My head snapped to the left, and there, parked beside the car in which I was currently sitting was my car.

Frantically, I clawed at the door handle, trying to escape. I managed to open the door and climb out in time to hear a familiar voice yell, "WHAT ARE YOU DOING IN MY CAR?" It was the same lady who had annoyed me so greatly by holding up my antacid purchase, walking towards me and shaking her finger in the air.

"I, uhhhhh, I got in your car by mistake," I said weakly, moving rapidly towards my own car. "I'm very sorry!"

Jumping inside my car, I started it quickly and backed out of my parking spot. The motor-mouthed lady was still standing on the sidewalk in front of her car. Her mouth was still making what looked like very angry words. But I knew I had to get out of there quickly. Little did she know that my mistake getting into her car was the least of her worries, and that awaiting her inside the vehicle was one of the worst atomic gas bombs I had ever detonated. As I peeled away, I just caught a glimpse of the lady sitting down in her driver's seat and closing the door. I felt bad for her.

To get back out on the main road to head towards my house, I had to drive to the opposite side of the parking lot and exit onto a small drive that took me right back past the front of the drug store parking lot. The lady was now standing outside of her car, bent over in a retching-vomiting posture.

All the way home, I feared being pulled over and arrested for the gas assault of the unfortunate lady from the drug store. I tried to ease my conscience by telling myself that she simply got what she deserved for being so selfish in the checkout line. But when I remembered how putrid the smell was that I left in her car, it was obvious that her punishment far out-weighed her crime.

57. WILL I HAVE I DONE WELL?

Am I doing well? When my children have grown and begin taking the steps that will become their journey through life, will I have done enough? Will I have passed or failed?

Should I have been more of an enforcer? Should I have been less of a tyrant? Did my own life, through their eyes, reflect the character I tried to instill within them? How many times should I have gone outside to play with those eager, smiling faces instead of being "too tired right now?" How many times did I miss the point they were trying to make because they only had my partial attention?

Can I claim victory if they don't end up on drugs or in prison? Have I failed if they don't become a doctor, or climb a corporate ladder to an office on the top floor? What if they end up an addict with a personality that is an inspiration to everyone around them? What if they earn millions of dollars, but are self-centered and uncaring towards others? How do I measure success as a father?

I look at people who seem to be very sensible and loving moms and dads, yet they have not talked to a son or daughter in many years, and it scares me. I don't have the courage to ask them if they could have done anything different. Have I done things that have widened the gap between parent and child?

I guess if there is one thing that I do know it's that there are no easy or definite answers to the fearful questions of a parent. There is no meter on the wall that tells us our current parenting skill rating. There is no book with the answers in the back that we can sneak peeks at. But then, if there were such things, maybe we wouldn't devote so much time and effort into trying to get it right.

I think we sometimes view child raising like it's an event. It seems like something that should have a start and an end, at which point we are either declared a winner or a loser. But as time with my kids goes on, I realize that this just isn't the case. There is no ending. I will be a dad until the day I die. My duties may change as they take control of their own lives, but I will never, not be their dad. I will never be completely free of responsibility or worry.

And maybe there is no victory or defeat. Maybe raising a child isn't a competition that we either win or lose. It is an ongoing relationship that both parent and child are trying to both enjoy and survive. When our kids are doing well, it can be tempting to say, "I win!" But that victory could be taken away between today and tomorrow. There is no point at which we can say, "I've done well enough," and then relax.

Likewise, we can look back and realize that we are doing poorly. We can identify mistakes we have made and learn from them. But I have to believe that there is no point at which we can say, "I have lost." There is only, "I need to try harder."

Jon Ziegler

THE CAST OF CHARACTERS

Jon (the author): Husband to Cynthia and father to Hannah and Natalie. Jon has spent most of his life as a tree trimmer or tower climber. His writing is done in spare time or when off work due to one of several shoulder surgeries. He also loves to cartoon, draw and wood work.

Cynthia: Wife of Jon, mother to Hannah and Natalie. Cynthia is a Registered Nurse (which comes in handy when married to a tree trimmer and have two rambunctious daughters). She is usually the organizer, planner and information gatherer. She makes sure that all school functions, doctors and dentist appointments, and every other important thing that involves numbers, dates, and paper work gets done on time. She has the unique gift of being one of the few people on earth who is able to put up with Jon as a husband.

Hannah: Oldest daughter of Jon and Cynthia, sister to Natalie, Hannah is a straight 'A' student who is heading off to college next fall armed with several academic scholarships. At this point, she is moving in the direction of an engineering degree. She is the dog lover in the house. Hannah also loves to read and is very artistic. Her dad is proud of some of her classic rock music choices as well.

Natalie: Youngest daughter of Jon and Cynthia, sister to Hannah, Natalie has had a horse listed as her number one item on her Christmas list since she has been able to write the word. She is the cat lover in the house and owner of nearly every rodent who has resided with us. Natalie is very artistic as well. Her dad is not as big of a fan of her Hip Hop music choices, but does enjoy making up his own substitute lyrics to the songs.

Together, we love, fight, cry, and most importantly, laugh our way through life. We are not a perfect family by any stretch of the word. But it can honestly be said that we all care for each other, and truly enjoy our time here on earth together.

From Inside the Brain of a Dad Looking Out

Printed in Great Britain
by Amazon.co.uk, Ltd.,
Marston Gate.